THE SPENCERS
ON SPAS

THE SPENCERS ON SPAS

Raine Spencer

with photographs by

John Spencer

Weidenfeld and Nicolson
London

Dedicated to
Sir Henry Marking KCVO M.C.
Chairman of the British Tourist Authority
with affection and gratitude

Above Children in the Valley Gardens, Harrogate
Frontispiece View of Bath from Prior Park
Half title Front door in Oxford Parade, Cheltenham

ISBN 0 297 78310 6

Designed by Simon Bell for
George Weidenfeld and Nicolson
91 Clapham High Street
London SW4

Printed in Great Britain by
W.S. Cowell Ltd, Ipswich.

CONTENTS

The author is deeply grateful to The Buxton Water Company,
a subsidiary of Canada Dry Rawlings Limited,
for their generous sponsorship of this book.

All the author's royalties will be given to the Spa Towns
to restore wrought iron and other architectural features.

The Pavilion, Buxton, by Edward Milner, 1871

THE SPA TOWNS

INTRODUCTION

In Xanadu did Kubla Khan
A stately pleasure-dome decree:
Where Alph, the sacred river, ran
Through caverns measureless to man
   Down to a sunless sea.
So twice five miles of fertile ground
With walls and towers were girdled round:
And there were gardens bright with sinuous rills,
Where blossomed many an incense-bearing tree;
And here were forests ancient as the hills,
Enfolding sunny spots of greenery.

Samuel Taylor Coleridge

SCIENCE AND TECHNOLOGY have spoilt many of our fairy-stories. The man in the moon has never seemed to be the same smiling father-figure since the invention of spacecraft and satellites. I remember sitting in the nursery to watch the historic moon-walk of Neil Armstrong on television, while my small children, unimpressed by this impossible dream, implored me to switch to the other channel as they were missing their favourite lunch-time serial.

Water, however, in all its manifestations, has retained its mystery and its independence. If the sirens who tempted Ulysses and the Argonauts no longer exist, modern sailors still look for good omens which denote a lucky ship. The unavailing efforts of King Canute to turn back the sea, in the manner of a Dali painting, served to emphasise the strength of his adversary. Unexplained tidal waves still engulf the promenades of coastal resorts, and floods are a constant threat to the Fenlands. In Florence, the freak tides of 1966 caused the Arno to break its barrage, force open doors of churches and palaces and swirl into ground floors and basements, breaking statues and works of art.

Nevertheless, water remains an essential element of survival. The compelling need for potable water drew the earliest settlers to the banks of the Euphrates and the Nile, a far cry from the Aswan Dam. The Pont du Gard was emulated by aqueducts all over Europe, and nowadays it is taken for granted that water must be harnessed to provide hydro-electric power, or diverted for leisure into lakes and canals.

The reservoirs of the Elan Valley in Wales can service millions of people in Birmingham and the West Midlands, yet you are conscious of a dangerous primeval force as you watch the surging water plunge over the dams to join the river hundreds of feet below.

It was the same instinct of fear and awe which prompted the Romans in Bath to placate the Gods by throwing brooches, coins and gold bracelets into the spring. For good measure they added curses against their enemies written backwards upon scrolls of lead. In Malvern, St Ann's Well was used by early missionaries to baptise their converts to Christianity. At Buxton, the well was sealed by an emissary of Cromwell, determined to stamp out idolatry, who confiscated the crutches and votive offerings left in gratitude for the Saint. The chalybeate waters of Tunbridge Wells were said to engender fertility, so were repeatedly tried by Queen Catherine of Braganza, and the brine baths of Droitwich were credited with miraculous cures for cholera.

Legend and superstition thus surrounded the wells in all parts of Britain, and pilgrims travelled from far afield to alleviate their rheumatism, dropsy, disorders of the blood or 'melancholike humours'.

Private individuals and local managements soon saw an opportunity to attract customers and revenues, so hamlets blossomed into towns, villages were transformed into cities, and in the seventeenth and eighteenth centuries the Beau Monde arrived to patronise the hastily erected hotels, pump rooms, assembly rooms or lending libraries, and to attend balls, concerts and other divertissements. Their camp-followers were artistes, modistes, charlatans, entertainers, tricksters, supplicants, and the bourgeoisie, for all the world like the *levée* of the Marschallin in *Der Rosenkavalier*.

Spas were *in*. Lord Byron and the Duke of Wellington visited Cheltenham. The Prince Regent drove over from Warwick to admire the handsome new buildings of Leamington Spa. Princess Victoria rode up the Malvern Hills on a donkey named Royal Moses, and Charles Dickens poked fun at earnest young men running down the hills to improve their constitution.

The discipline and the amusements of spa towns attracted George Bernard Shaw and even Mrs Pankhurst, who caused pandemonium in Strathpeffer when she expounded there upon the equality of the sexes. Later in the century, Lloyd George, bent on more serious business than taking the waters, wrestled with the Italo-Abyssinian problem in Llandrindod Wells, frustrated by an old-fashioned telephone and an inadequate ledge for taking notes.

Today you cannot fail to be impressed by the gardens, the trees and the distinguished buildings of all periods in the spas, but there the similarity ends. Some are hubs of activity and entertainment. Others are quiet, sleepy places where you can re-charge your batteries and mentally set the world to rights.

In writing this book I was stimulated by the historical connections which emerged during our travels; by other links which existed between some of the towns, and by finding unexpected architectural treasures in the surrounding villages and countryside. Cottages, churches, mills, cathedrals, manor houses or palaces were often associated with people who had changed the course of history, or achieved fame and fortune from humble beginnings.

This is a personal story of our visits to British spas, which I hope you will have time to discover for yourself.

CHELTENHAM SPA

THE FIRST TIME I went to Cheltenham was with Granny Cartland. It was just after the war ended, and it was a major outing. Granny drove at some speed, as she always did, burning the carefully saved-up petrol, talking nineteen to the dozen. There was little competition on the roads in those days, as we went through Hanley Swan and Hanley Castle, over the bridge at Upton-on-Severn, over the border to Gloucestershire. Granny would regale me with stories of her youth, how she bicycled to tennis parties, her long dress pinned up to protect it from the wheels, or to grand receptions at Croome Court, long before the pink Tapestry Room was sold lock, stock, and barrel to the Metropolitan. She used to tell me about Worcester, where there were several dubious alleys, one in particular called Bull Entry, where drunken husbands beat their wives on Saturday nights, and where children begged bare-foot in the streets.

Cheltenham was different. Cheltenham was respectable. Aunts or cousins or widowers of Granny's friends lived there in the upright Regency houses. They played contract bridge with retired colonels who had been posted to far-flung parts of the British Empire. As young subalterns they heard talk in the Mess of the times when Lord Curzon had rebuilt the Viceroy's house at Delhi, and had caused the cleaning and restoration of the Taj Mahal.

Granny's friends' relations went shopping in the Promenade and skated in the winter on Pittville Lake; some had even attended the opening of the splendid new Town Hall in 1903.

Our own Mecca was Cavendish House. There are charming old photographs of shoppers with the huge bell skirts of the 1850s, holding parasols, walking down the Promenade in front of this famous department store. Top-hatted gentlemen peer into the windows, a horse trots past the gas lantern, and another man, of a more artistic appearance, hands in pockets, strolls beneath the striped awnings.

To this day, Cavendish House is a shop where all kinds of tempting goods are proffered by salespersons who really do seem to care whether you buy or not. Granny used to buy gloves, and sometimes a hat for a wedding, and coffee sugar on a string like brown glass which had to be hammered into a suitable size for small cups. We used to meet friends who had come in from the county for the same purpose. To my astonishment, when I returned to Cavendish House after

Window canopies in Oxford Parade

thirty-five years, a woman rushed up to me in the perfumery who turned out to be a childhood friend.

Granny had decided to give me a special present. I had been afflicted by mumps, a distinctly anti-social disease, and had been hastily packed off away from my small brothers. I was sixteen, in that no-man's land of girlhood, and Granny wanted to make me feel grown-up and important. We went to the counter which sold brushes and manicure sets, and there, unbelievably, was the most beautiful dressing-table set in the world, blue enamel on silver, with not only brushes and clothes brushes galore, but cut-glass pots and bottles topped with the same blue enamel, nail files, a shoe horn and even a button-hook for long white gloves. This treasure was encased in blue morocco leather, a suitcase so precious that it had its own protective cover. Nowadays anyone carrying it would have a heart attack long before reaching even the Eurolounge of Heathrow Airport – but in those days it still seemed possible to use such glamorous appurtenances.

Granny gave it to me; and Cheltenham for me is forever associated with that wonderful present, which today rests on a dressing-table hung with frilled white muslin in a State Bedroom at Althorp, my husband's house, complementing the silver-framed mirror which belonged to Sarah, Duchess of Marlborough. All the visitors think that my present from Cheltenham must be a Spencer heirloom.

Today Cheltenham is no longer associated with colonels, and even the connection with the famous Ladies' College, where pupils are still groomed for stardom in the many professions now open to women, is less talked about than two manifestations of the twentieth century – technology and spying. The two are often inter-connected, since industrial espionage does not only occur in James Bond films.

In 1931, George Dowty, with a capital of £50, rented a mews loft in Cheltenham and started to make internally-sprung aircraft wheels. Friends who had garages or back gardens helped out with extra work, and this remarkable company now exports all over the world hydraulic equipment, propellers, fuel systems and other ancillary requirements for aircraft. This enterprise has given substantial employment to the area. It has brought businessmen to buy and to spend nights in the many hotels in the town. Eagle Star Insurance, Kraft Cheese, Gulf Oil and Smiths Industries are other important companies which have found a new home in Cheltenham. They have provided a financial balance between the traditional artistic activities, such as the international festivals of music and literature, the yearly speech and drama festival with its 8,000 competitors, the orchestras, recitals and the theatre, and the need for solid rateable values in a town which spends over £350,000 a year on restoring its 1,700 listed historic buildings.

A few months ago someone told me 'We have more spies in Cheltenham than Cambridge'. That is not really difficult, since, in the familiar terminology of spy stories, many of those seemingly innocent Professors or the old-time Cambridge roués have had their covers blown . The Government Communications Headquarters, as it is whimsically called, is a modern building, designed with restraint, and architecturally not unlike the American Express building at Brighton. From time to

Bandstand in Pittville Gardens

time scandals erupt, and one longs to know just where the 'drops' were made, where those chance encounters took place. Did the trusted few, imbued with a desire for transient fame or money, or motivated by misguided idealism, manage to transfer to Ivan or Boris or Leonid the secret ingredient of the newest underwater radar, or the antidote which can deflect the Exocet missile, or even a lot of rubbish if they were double-agents after all?

Reality and fiction often steer a parallel course. Yet there are no more chases through the sewers of Vienna as in *The Third Man*, or sinister meetings beside the merry-go-round in the Prater, merely the casual walk across Hampstead Heath or Wandsworth Common, the little parcel carefully taped inside the hollow tree, or delivered to the sleazy individual in the pornographic bookshop. How, then, does this fit in with Cheltenham?

Did the casual encounters take place in the lounge of the handsome Queen's Hotel, built in 1838, which dominates the end of the Promenade and resembles classical buildings in old St Petersburg? Was the Victorian letter-box in Malvern Place, cast in iron at Dudley, Worcestershire, the silent recipient of secrets designed to facilitate the overthrow of our long-established civilisation? Did the blue-and-white bandstand on the sloping lawns beyond Pittville Pump Room have microfilm taped to the back of the Chinese fret of its balustrade, or was the information rather more cheekily tucked into one of the window-boxes of marigolds and lobelia outside the Municipal Offices?

We will never know. We will equally never know the real reason behind the act. Dame Rebecca West, in *The Meaning of Treason*, has explained better than anyone else the psychology of traitors, but whilst one can feel sympathy with those who are blackmailed for some transgression, or, as is so often the case, beguiled by a brief flowering of physical love for a foreign diplomat, or for their own complicated and twisted set of ideals, agree to take part in this charade, one cannot forgive them for knowingly putting at risk the lives of innocent civilians, or men and women on active service.

But enough of these diversions. We have come to Cheltenham to enjoy ourselves. How should we begin? Let us begin in the Promenade, just by the Obelisk, where the hanging baskets of flowers, the trees, the shops and the feeling of space on the wide pavements make one understand why, in the early nineteenth century, this was the grand walk up towards Sherborne Spa. This was the obligatory constitutional, before imbibing the spa waters, where friends were encountered, invitations offered, flirtations started, and where you might easily see Lord Byron or the Duke of Wellington riding by to visit friends on neighbouring estates, or the Duke of Gloucester, a regular visitor, who entertained his niece, Princess Victoria, in the August of 1830.

Today we are still impressed, as were Dr Johnson and Lord Dartmouth in the 1750s, by the quality and elegance of the buildings in the town. Americans often say: 'We do love your intimate little houses – they look so cosy.' What they really mean is that the scale of eighteenth- and early nineteenth-century English domestic architecture is entirely livable-in, is not garish or fussy, and does not overwhelm or intimidate the inhabitants.

Kenneth Clark once remarked that we live in the age of brutalism, and brutal architecture is the inevitable result. Alas, for our towns and cities. Monstrous carbuncles of concrete have erupted in gentle Georgian Squares. The 1950s fashion for high-rise swept away acres of friendly terraced streets, and trendy architects entirely ignored the understandable wish of mothers to watch their small children playing outside, obviously impossible twenty-one storeys above ground. It was not until old ladies became continually terrorised by young thugs in lifts defaced by graffiti, until young wives committed suicide from fear and loneliness in isolated flats, until Ronan Point actually collapsed, that local authorities and the powers-that-be decided to reverse their previous policies and refurbish and modernise older properties.

Modern architecture can be stunning in the right setting. In Rio de Janeiro and Hong Kong, both of which have a backdrop of mountains to set off their sky-scrapers; in New York, where the Seagram and General Motors buildings create an immediate sense of drama; in New Rome, Italy; and anywhere in the world where one can find the work of Professor Nervi. A striking example is his field-house at Dartmouth College, New Hampshire, with its roof of delicately

Wrought-iron balconies in the town

worked interlaced concrete, reminiscent of the flying buttresses of an old cathedral. But in England, despite a small percentage of outstanding work which has actually enhanced the environment, the greater part of the modern architecture we see around us is regrettably intrusive, ugly, thoughtless, selfish and an utter disaster.

In contrast, the Municipal Offices of Cheltenham, on the Promenade, have been described as one of the great terraces of Europe. Built between 1818 and 1826, it has happily survived and been lovingly restored. Further along in St George's Road, where there are window canopies, and exquisite wrought iron on the balconies, the houses have been deliberately made smaller, and the road wider, to create a perspective which is both subtle and dramatic, leading gradually up an incline to the Corinthian columns of the Queen's Hotel, where once you were faced with the cannon, aligned for decorative purposes only, which were used by our troops at Sebastopol.

To the right, on the corner of Montpellier Parade, is Morgans, grocers and wine merchants. The traditional façade is black with gold lettering, and they are renowned for good service and unusual epicurean delights. Beyond, marking the start of Montpellier Parade, is the National Westminster Bank, cleaned and cared for, as are so many banks now housed in historic buildings all over the country, for which we should offer heartfelt thanks. Without the directors' sense of responsibility towards the many beautiful buildings which have sometimes been inconvenient and difficult to convert for everyday use, our towns and cities would be much the poorer.

Montpellier Walk is one of the star turns of Cheltenham. A continuous line of small arcaded shops is intersected by caryatids: strange, remote ladies, of painted terracotta with swathed heads, in some ways reminiscent of the bronze sibyls of seventeenth-century Italy. These figures with truncated arms support on their heads the entablature, with its motif of oak leaves, which draws together this exclusive enclave where antiques, a tea-room, several boutiques and a restaurant are all watched over by these inscrutable guardians.

When the street was lined with trees, the band used to play in front of Montpellier Pump Room. Built in 1817, it is now Lloyds Bank. The colonnaded front, surmounted by a stone lion guarding a flagpole, with the huge rotunda behind, used to denote the entrance to this meeting place for the Beau Monde. It was one of the earliest of Cheltenham's many spas, commissioned by a banker, Henry Thompson.

At right angles to Montpellier Walk is Montpellier Terrace, where the Spa Pharmacy to this day sports a giant gilded pestle and mortar above the front entrance, and one can envisage ladies dropping in to purchase medicines and lavender water, or a restorative should they be overcome by faintness during a concert or assembly. One of the more doubtful pleasures was the fashionable Public Breakfast, which at least took place at mid-day, unlike the uncivilised working breakfasts at 8 a.m. attended by politicians and businessmen today.

Just round the corner, and running parallel to the Parade, is the less well-known Montpellier Street. Here there are simple Regency houses with tiny shops below overflowing with tempting wares. The Salad Bowl is a riot of bright vegetables, and you can find curios, furniture, clothes and presents of every description. In the arcade which links Montpellier Street to the Parade, a corner shop called Cocoa sells antique lace and the proprietor leaves a pram on the pavement as an advertisement. There is a wine bar and a bistro, and as you continue down the street, every now and then beyond the curving frontages there is a tantalising view of the Cotswold hills, a reminder that this sophisticated town is in the heart of the Gloucestershire countryside.

One of the most beautiful groups of buildings in Cheltenham is the Lansdowns – Crescent, Terrace, and Parade. It is curious how often this name recurs in the spa towns, as in Bath, and in Leamington where there are Lansdownes, with an 'e', which are also 'ensembles' of the Georgian period. Cheltenham's Lansdown

Houses in Oxford Parade

Crescent, a convex sweep of houses, with the wrought iron painted in green, has been restored in a combined effort costing £4 million by the Borough Council and the Guinness Trust. The Historic Buildings Council has given a substantial grant, and this classical group, where paired front doors have porches supported by columns, is a foil to Landsdown Parade, on the other side of the green, where the two-storey houses with Greek Doric porches and wide windows to the reception

Above and opposite The Pittville Pump Room

rooms are at once formal yet lacking in pomposity, and are linked into a complete façade by the central house with its triangular pediment.

Lansdown Terrace, my own favourite, is more elaborate. Designed by the Jearrad brothers, who did so much work in Cheltenham, each house has a classical portico to the main room on the first floor, with pairs of Ionic columns supporting a pediment rising from a stone balcony. There is an Italian feeling, faint echoes of Vicenza, but everything is scaled down to make certain that these are houses in which families or single people can live and work, according to their needs, yet animate buildings which are part of the continuity of the town.

And so it is with Oxford Parade. These are the buildings I am most fond of, despite the vast choice in Cheltenham. In 1975, when I was Chairman for the United Kingdom of European Architectural Heritage Year, I was asked to formally open the houses which had just been restored. It had not been an easy task, for despite the dry rot and decay, there were tenants who did not want to move, even temporarily, and some who would not even allow the frontages to be cleaned at no cost to themselves. During the ceremony a furious man delivered a diatribe to the Mayor on the iniquities of Council interference. After eighteen years in Local Government I know only too well the problems facing local authorities, and one could not help but laugh at the paradox of the unfortunate Council having to ward off the brickbats of rampant conservationists, allay the suspicions of irate ratepayers about wasting money on old buildings, and at the same time placate angry tenants who were apparently quite happy to sit doing nothing while the houses fell about their ears.

Oxford Parade is built of that glowing, faintly apricot-coloured Cotswold stone. Some front doors are painted brownish-red, and the window-guards are of the most delicate wrought iron, with criss-cross work at the top and bottom. This pattern is repeated on the wrought iron of the porches with their pagoda tops, which give the impression that they are only fragile tents put out to protect a visiting Chinese dignitary from the sunshine. Above the first-floor windows are more serious pagodas with wrought iron descending along the edge like a criss-cross fringe. Yet they seem so light and insubstantial that one wants to carry them off on a stick, and whirl them round as a chorus member of *Turandot*, while Birgit Nilsson, wearing Cecil Beaton's costume with its vast train, descends the long staircase from the temple of the Forbidden City on the stage at Covent Garden, her hands almost imprisoned by the long, cruel, false finger-nails, singing those soaring arias exulting in the untimely deaths of her princely lovers.

Such nasty habits would soon have been nipped in the bud had Princess Turandot been sent to Cheltenham Ladies' College. One of the most famous schools in England, it was founded in 1853 to provide an education based on Christian precepts, and for fifty years from 1856 it was guided by a remarkable principal, Dorothea Beale. She gave her pupils an education which was both sensible and cultural, encouraged extensive reading in the library which today houses no less than 22,000 volumes, and in general promoted the emancipation of women.

Caroline Herschel, Elizabeth Fry and Mary Somerville were all products of the nineteenth century, and until that time, with notable exceptions such as Queen Elizabeth I and girls of noble families who were taught alongside their brothers by resident tutors, the education of women was sadly neglected during the Dark Ages of Europe right up until the onset of the Industrial Revolution. Yet in ancient Athens and Rome, women had been educated as carefully as men. The revival of serious educational establishments for women in the nineteenth century made possible the gradual change of public opinion which today means that there are women judges, barristers, bank managers, deaconesses, pilots and computer operators. At a recent luncheon in honour of celebrated women I met a Nobel Prize winner, the scientist Dr Dorothy Hodgkin, introduced to me by a friend who also possesses both brains and charm, the gynaecologist Dame Josephine Barnes. In 1853, men would have laughed to scorn the very idea of such achievements.

In 1983, the College buildings needed for science, for the language laboratory, for the pottery and textile department and for the girls to live in, have spread into many different parts of Cheltenham, including Bayshill Road, where George III and his family spent a five-week holiday in 1788. The buildings themselves, mostly Victorian Gothic, are by Middleton, Prothero and Robson, designed or enlarged at various intervals as the needs of pupils developed, and the science laboratory by Tait and Ault, built in 1960, is luckily of low scale in this street of Regency villas.

The girls of the College still carry off many of the top scholarships at Oxford or Cambridge. A friend of mine, while she was a pupil, enjoyed the various arts activities, and when she left worked for many years in a leading art gallery. When pressed to tell me recollections of her schooldays, she instantly and enthusiastically remembered 'The wonderful green peppermint ice-cream at the Queen's Hotel, and at Cavendish House those high, cool glasses filled with knickerbocker glories'. Apparently a great deal of Cheltenham was out of bounds, and if rules were broken, there were always busy-bodies ready to report that the green uniform, with red piping on the belt, had been seen in an unaccustomed spot. My friend hated games, but liked history lessons, the walks round Hatherley, and going to concerts in Pittville Pump Room during the summer festival.

During the reign of Dorothea Beale, Lily Langtry came to Cheltenham to open the Opera House, emphasising the role of this Cotswold town as a cultural centre. Today the building is luckily not a bingo hall, but remains as the Everyman Theatre, a magnet for theatre-lovers who come from every part of Gloucestershire to enjoy a wide variety of plays. There is also the Cheltenham Playhouse for amateur productions, and the Festival of Literature in October attracts established poets, playwrights and novelists, and stimulates new work by providing a platform for aspiring writers.

Another aspect of Cheltenham is the ghosts. In Pittville Circus Road, a tall weeping woman continually haunted St Anne's House; in St Philip's Street, a man carrying a gas-mask and wearing clothes of 1914 regularly accosts pedestrians as he vainly searches for his dog; in Hatherley Road, a poltergeist ransacked the cutlery and knocked over stools in the kitchen, and a ghostly cavalier still rides on moonlit nights from Sudeley Castle bearing important despatches for Edward IV.

There could also be the ghosts of Dr Jenner, Fred Archer the jockey, Gilbert Laird Jessop, who made fifty-three centuries during his cricketing career, and Sir Frederick Handley Page, designer of the twin-engined bomber for the First World War. Lord Tennyson wrote *In Memoriam* at 10 St James's Square, and Sir Ralph Richardson, whose acting has given pleasure to millions through plays, films and television, was born in one of the classical nineteenth-century villas of Tivoli Road.

The list of Cheltenham's famous sons and daughters seems endless, and their achievements have merited world-wide acclaim.

The town was also visited by the world and his wife after the momentous discovery in 1716 of a spring with salt deposits near the Chelt. William Mason, the owner of the spring, had a daughter, Elizabeth, who married a merchant captain from Bristol, Henry Skillicorne; twenty years later it was he who installed a pumping system, built the Old Well and opened a list of subscribers.

Cheltenham was now all set to dispense the curative waters and to become a fashionable spa. Montpellier and Sherborne Spas followed until, by 1834, there were six major spas within the town. Warm or tepid baths, gentle exercise and daily drinking of the waters were prescribed to alleviate all kinds of dread and unmentionable diseases. Grand visitors began to pour into the town, to take houses for the season, to arrange to see friends and to demand entertainment in the form of balls, card parties, concerts and fireworks. Gala Fêtes would be staged which featured jugglers, trapeze artists and balloonists. There were the waxworks of Madame Tussaud, and recitals by Johann Strauss and the great maestro Paganini. There was a Master of Ceremonies to determine dress and behaviour and to vet applicants for these amusements, while at the theatre one could be entertained by Grimaldi the clown, Edmund Kean or Sarah Siddons. The Races were inaugurated in 1818, and the Cheltenham Gold Cup, still highly prized today, was run for the first time in 1819. What fun it must have been. If you were sated with social life, there were libraries, a museum and a picture gallery, and from 1840 onwards visitors could see important works by Holbein, Velázquez, Rubens and Titian belonging to Lord Northwick at Thirlestaine House.

The most attractive spa must always have been Pittville, and the Pump Room today, with its colonnade of Ionic columns copied from the Temple of Ilissus, its interior elliptical arches below the gallery, its dome encrusted with Greek paterae, and even a classical fountain where the water is still dispensed, stands as a reminder of all those festive occasions when there was boating on the lake and skating in the winter, and the band played the works of Strauss to amuse the ladies in their long muslin dresses as they took their promenade.

It is not a ruin, nor a neglected historic building, but has a Gallery of Fashion on the upper floor, and is repainted, revitalised and in constant use, for concerts, recitals and parties. The well-kept gardens in front of the lake are crowded in summer with residents or visitors enjoying one of the Festivals, taking a break from an Antiques Fair, or a short walk in between business appointments.

Nowadays the equivalent of taking the waters has become the sauna, the sunbed, the jacuzzi. There is slimming, swimming and hydrotherapy. Jogging has replaced the 'gentle exercise' recommended all those years ago. The hotels of Cheltenham offer many of these necessities or adjuncts to health, as well as delicious meals, attractive décor and sweeping views of the surrounding countryside. Often the

Garden of the Greenway

The Lilleybrook Hotel

Jacuzzi at Staverton Court

clever conversions have entailed the installation of boardrooms and conference rooms in Regency, Georgian or Victorian buildings which were once sizeable family homes, or manor houses on the outskirts of the town.

Once upon a time there was Saxon Cheltenham, near the Roman Fosse Way. There was Medieval Cheltenham, with a Thursday market, and a three-day agricultural fair each summer. Seventeenth-century Cheltenham widened its economy by the cultivation of tobacco, while the inhabitants still lived in thatched cottages with rear gardens and orchards. In the early eighteenth century the Plough Inn was the main feature of the High Street, and the Crescent, the Parade and the Promenade would still have been cloud-cuckoo land. Modern Cheltenham is an impressive, thriving Cotswold town. Yet it has a warm, robust, country feeling derived from its background as a market town where bull-baiting, cock-fighting and cudgel matches were the only amusements. It was a place where Susan Newsam might have been sold one Thursday as in Hardy's *Mayor of Casterbridge*. Yet after the discovery of the springs, kings and princesses were drawn by its fame to taste the waters, to admire the new classical buildings and to mingle with the dazzling, gorgeously-dressed aristocracy at one of the balls in the Assembly Rooms.

Nowadays the entertainments offered are still as exciting, but they are attended by a wider section of society. People of all ages, executives and tourists, come for education, for recreation, for business or holidays. The parks, the air, the food and the exercise can restore jaded palates and pale cheeks, reduce tension, revive the spirits, engender pleasure and romance. Where better to go than Cheltenham Spa?

WOODHALL SPA

IF YOU ARE TIRED of traffic, depressed by concrete office blocks, choked by diesel fumes, tormented by noisy towns and harassed by your fellow men, then Woodhall Spa in Lincolnshire is the perfect escape. As you turn the corner into the Broadway, where the small shops sport brightly-striped awnings, and where the comfortable low-built private houses give the residents quiet seclusion in the gardens enclosed by neatly cut beech hedges, you feel your cares fade away. It does not seem to matter that the pushy executive was trying to upstage you, and the argument in the canteen or the fuss over that late delivery of raw materials becomes a blurred memory as you catch sight of the magnificent privately-owned championship golf course, surrounded with bracken and yellow gorse, where larches, pines and silver birch trees enclose the first tee.

On our initial visit we got lost in the hinterland east of Stamford, and found ourselves in the Fens. It was a cold day in March, and suddenly we were on a straight narrow road, slightly raised above the surrounding fields. They were flat and appeared deserted, and the rich, dark soil seen in the clear light, the sparse villages, the occasional farmhouse, seemed to suggest a murder story in the tradition of Dorothy Sayers. Later, when the sun came through and illuminated the low, unbroken skyline, the Fens were part of a Philips de Koninck landscape, borrowed from our Dutch neighbours, not far away from Lincolnshire over the Hook of Holland.

It seemed as if we would never reach our destination, as when the straight road ended there were pack-horse bridges and tiny level crossings where the barrier had clanged down almost ten minutes before the train was due. I half expected to see sheep and cattle sitting in the road, so rural was the scene, but there was only a trailer full of potatoes and sugar beet, pulled by a tractor, to remind us that this deep soil made of silt from the Wash, a former inland lake, is the most productive farm-land in Europe.

Woodhall Spa is often described as an oasis, and coming from the flat Fen country into this riot of trees – Scots pines, oak, beech, and the long avenue of limes in the main street, one sees it as a mirage – the *mise-en-scène* for the last act of a pantomime, or the creation, perhaps, of the aptly named Miss Maple, later Lady Weigall, after whom Maple Avenue is named. Her handsome black-and-white half-timbered house, used during the war as the officers' Mess of the Dam Busters, is now the Petwood Hotel. It was also Lady Weigall who in 1920 gave to a war

The Kinema in the Woods

veteran the little black and cream pavilion on her estate which is now the enchanting 'Kinema in the Woods'. Residents of Woodhall Spa still remember watching the programmes from deck-chairs and benches. Now there are comfortable seats for several hundred people and interior decoration of imitation marble. The outside is still like the home of Hansel and Gretel. One expects a wooden girl and boy to swing in and out at intervals to denote fair weather or foul; one anticipates old Charlie Chaplin films, Walt Disney's *Fantasia*, or Valentino as the Sheik, to entertain us on the screen as perhaps they diverted the members of Lady Weigall's house parties during those evening performances which for her convenience were held a little later than usual. But the present cinematic fare caters for more modern tastes with films like *Annie*, *Poltergeist* and *Confessions of a Pop Performer*.

Healing wax in the Spa Baths   Signpost in the woods

Alongside in the woods is the popular Tea House with its arched frontage, where tables with umbrellas are crowded each summer with day visitors who come from Lincoln, Grimsby or Hull to play tennis, watch the bowls in Jubilee Park or fish for bream or perch on the river Witham. The Spa Baths, covered with red virginia creeper, are also nearby, where treatments prescribed on the National Health Service were available until 1982. Over the years water from the spring discovered in 1824 has alleviated thousands of cases of gout and rheumatism.

An intriguing sight in Woodhall Spa is the Wellington Monument, a tall obelisk surmounted by a bust of the Iron Duke, standing in a field outside a wood planted from acorns sown in 1815 to commemorate the battle of Waterloo. Another monument of greater antiquity is the mysterious Toro-Mor, a fragment of a tower said to have been the shooting lodge of Tattershall Castle, erected in the fifteenth century by Lord Cromwell, Treasurer to Henry VI. But the most striking feature of this small town is the architecture of the 1900s, rows of charming gabled houses with recurring black-and-white motifs on their upper storeys which echo the style set by the dramatic Golf Hotel, framed by silver birch trees. There is the Gamecock, a half-timbered public house, the red-brick Methodist church in the Broadway, the Victorian Post Office in Clarence Road, and sudden glimpses of the Viking Way, the long-distance footpath for keen walkers which links Humberside to Leicestershire.

In Horncastle Road the cleverly sited holiday chalets of Bainland Park, with a background of mature trees, have steeply pitched roofs and are fashioned of warm red cedar planks fitted in a diagonal design. Tennis, ping-pong and a nine-hole golf course, as well as saunas, a jacuzzi and an indoor swimming pool, provide relaxation for visitors.

Everywhere you look in Woodhall Spa the impression of quiet and privacy is emphasised by the tall hedges of beech or hawthorn, a profusion of hydrangeas and rhododendrons, and the pine trees with their faint, tangy smell of resin.

Only about eighteen miles to the north-west is Lincoln, one of the most beautiful capital cities in England. As we drove through the outskirts, we could see through the December mist the twin towers of the Cathedral, consecrated in 1092, which on the high plateau above Steep Hill, dominates every other building.

In Minster Yard, one first becomes aware of its vast proportions and of the breathtaking thirteenth-century west front with towers flanked by corner turrets. Eleven crowned kings from William the Conqueror to Edward III in a frieze over the splendid Norman doorway anticipate the grandeur of the interior. For there you find arch upon arch, column upon column, surmounted by the soaring vaulted roof of the nave instigated by St Hugh of Avalon, born in France near Grenoble, Bishop of Lincoln in 1186, whose symbol was a swan. Today swans still glide gracefully down the river Witham, beneath the arch of the High Bridge, to remind us of that Norman saint who was canonised only twenty years after his death.

When I entered the Cathedral, the sun shining through the bright blue and red glass of the south windows threw a kaleidoscope of colour onto the stone pillars opposite, and illuminated one of the side aisles. In the south transept the circular window of 1220, called the 'Bishop's Eye', has stained glass in gentler colours, and beneath the choir-stalls are the curious misericords which depict a variety of different personalities including Tristan and Isolde, Samson and Delilah, and Alexander the Great. The monuments include the tombchest of Bartholomew, Lord Burghersh, guarded by four angels, two of whom hold his soul in a napkin. Sometimes in the winter months the Cathedral resounds to the strains of Handel's *Messiah*, performed by the London Mozart Players. On other occasions music lovers can hear the cellist Julian Lloyd-Webber.

Outside again in Minster Yard, where small Georgian houses face the Cathedral, you pass through the arch of the fourteenth-century Exchequergate and walk for a few moments backwards in time to medieval Lincoln. Facing you is the battlemented outline of Lincoln Castle, and on the right-hand corner the black-and-white timbered merchant's house with its sloping front and entrance in Bailgate. On the left are the cobbles of Steep Hill, where one would not be surprised to see clerks warmly wrapped in cloaks hurrying by with samples of wool to show to buyers from Holland who would then export their purchases from Boston, once one of the busiest ports in England. In Steep Hill you can find little shops for books, jewellery and antiques; there is a wood parlour; and the Wig and Mitre, a public house and eating place where above the stairs the old rafters reinforced with rushes are still visible behind glass. Further down there is the Norman House, and in Michaelgate a tiny, crooked house, half timbered and half red brick, which has sweeping views of the Vale of Belvoir. Just as we reached almost the oldest part of this fascinating area interspersed with Victorian lanterns, a Vulcan Bomber soared past, in order, perhaps, to emphasise that only three miles away is RAF Waddington, and that one of the largest employers in Lincoln today is Marconi, which produced the Radar system used in the Falklands conflict.

The lower part of Steep Hill is called the Strait, and here shop signs are permitted to hang out over the road, creating at once a feeling of intimacy as in the Getreidegasse of Salzburg, or in Hong Kong where Chinese banners advertise the myriad jewellery shops in Kowloon.

In the busy pedestrianised High Street the Halifax Building Society is housed in the Cardinal's Hat, named after Wolsey, Chancellor to Henry VIII and builder of Hampton Court, who somehow found time to be Bishop of Lincoln in 1514. The Stonebow of 1605 is still the main meeting place for the townsfolk, who can shelter in rainy weather beneath its arches. Immediately above is the Guildhall, its stone façade adorned with a Tudor rose and the fleur-de-lys of Lincoln, where every six weeks the Councillors are summoned to a special session by the Mote Bell, the oldest in the country. Further along, in the widest part of the street, Marks and Spencer are evident in a handsome building of the 1930s which blends surprisingly well with its restored Tudor neighbour, and with the various seventeenth- and eighteenth-century buildings of this part of the city. Just here the High Bridge spans the river, and while we had coffee in a first-floor café, we could see the fish barge moored near Cornhill Market where every day fresh fish from Grimsby is for sale.

Fountain at Bainland Park

The Golf Hotel

This unusual city, where the many sixteenth-century timbered merchants' houses remain a tribute to their owners' hard work and financial acumen, and where today Ruston, a leading local firm, make turbines for the oil-rigs off Aberdeen and parts for the Siberian Gas Pipeline across Russia, has proved that it is possible to adapt to the needs of the twentieth century yet retain not only the atmosphere, but also the beauty of the past. When my husband was in South Australia, he travelled to Port Lincoln, discovered during the Napoleonic Wars by Matthew Flinders, the explorer from Lincolnshire. Since that time the Lincolnshire names of Cape Donnington, Boston Isles, Spalding Cove, and Sleaford Mere have a dual role as towns or lagoons in the Antipodes.

Another worthwhile outing from Woodhall Spa is to Louth. On Wednesdays there are stalls in the eighteenth-century Cornmarket which sell home-made butter, plants, cut flowers and, in season, rabbits, pheasants and partridges. Just behind is the covered market, with shops on the perimeter, and stalls in the centre. Business is brisk and there is a wide choice, as in the larger nineteenth-century covered markets of Leeds and Budapest, in both of which the architects have shown consideration for shoppers in a cold climate, and also supplied a certain charm notably lacking in the claustrophobic modern shopping precincts of today.

Market towns seem to have their own special character. If you ask passers-by about market day, they reply with a lilt in their voice which denotes that it is still a social occasion from time immemorial, when pedlars mingled with the crowds to sell ribbons and favours for pretty girls, and charlatans like Dr Dulcamara in *Elisir d'Amore* would proffer bottles and powders which purported for a few pence to effect miraculous cures. What an adventure it must have been to drive some fifteen miles in the dray laden with produce, and return with it almost empty, having made a few purchases of other men's goods, struck some satisfactory deals or exchanges, drunk draught beer or cider in the local inn, and, if you were young and single, encountered a pair of laughing eyes, or followed up the invitation of a glimpse of frilled petticoat beneath a cambric dress.

In the market place of Horncastle, there is an imposing Victorian memorial of carved stone and granite, at first sight almost an Eleanor Cross, which was put up by public subscription to Edward Stanhope, the Member of Parliament from 1874 to 1893. How few politicians nowadays achieve fame which is so permanent and so expensive, right in the centre of the town, for it is here that the market is held on a Thursday. As a complementary background, there is an upright Georgian building, now the Post Office; a shop for guns and cartridges which has crossed Enfield rifles of 1858 above the entrance, and a stationer and newsagent whose arched windows, outlined in Regency wrought iron, have 'Swan Fountain Pens' and 'Swan Ink' advertised in the original black and gold lettering. The owner told me that his father had bought the shop in 1920, and that it once belonged to a milliner. I can imagine bonnets trimmed with curling feathers, ribbons or flowers making a ravishing display to tempt farmers' wives or daughters on their shopping expeditions to this charming small town set in the undulating countryside of this part of Lincolnshire.

Between Louth and Horncastle, almost hidden in a maze of tiny, twisting lanes, is the hamlet of Somersby. It was here that Tennyson was born, in a low, rambling Georgian house, now painted a very pale pink. There is a large bell at one side of the front door, and at the rear one can see for miles over the fields in the clear light. It is now privately owned and not open to the public, but there is always a curious fascination about places where great men were born, and the system of Blue Plaques which are on so many houses in London, is one of the most popular activities of the Greater London Council. I remember well going to The Pheasantry, in the Kings Road, to see Anton Dolin and Alicia Markova unveil a plaque to their ballet teacher, the Russian Princess Serafin Astafieva. It was touching to learn how her tuition of artists who subsequently became famous has resulted in countless hours of happiness for audiences all round the world. I remember also standing outside No. 88, Mile End Road, while heavy lorries thundered past, almost drowning the voice of the Australian High Commissioner during his speech about Captain Cook; and I remember making a special journey to see the birthplace of Benjamin Disraeli in that humble house in Theobalds Road, Holborn.

Tennyson must have been inspired by his Lincolnshire background, and especially by the area round Somersby, where his father was Rector. His statue in Lincoln by G. F. Watts in 1905 portrays him with a dog and a broad-brimmed hat. Later his widowed mother moved with her children to Cheltenham, a busy, fashionable town, and one can hardly imagine a greater contrast to the quiet of Somersby, whose nearest neighbour, Ashby Puerorum, is an even smaller hamlet, just a farm and two or three houses, and holds the unusual name from the fact that the living was appropriated to support the choirboys of Lincoln Cathedral.

Returning to Woodhall Spa, a few miles south of the town lies Tattershall Castle. It is a strange relic of the time when Ralph, Lord Cromwell, was Treasurer of England, and it must always have dominated the surrounding fenland. It exudes menace. One thinks of Macbeth. Even the civilising influence of the fireplaces, decorated with elaborate coats of arms, and saved from speculators by Lord Curzon, when he bought and restored the building in 1911, cannot entirely convince one that this apparently residential tower was anything more than a fortified keep, where archers waited at upper windows to repel raiders, or other henchmen were busy with the boiling oil.

But enough of historic buildings, however interesting. Next I must take you to Skegness, to the sea – but not to the lonely sea – to all the fun of the sands and the donkey rides and the lights. To the gardens, the bowling greens, the fireworks; to the discos, the cabarets and the amusement parks. Some friends of mine who have relatives at Skegness and go there on holiday every summer say they would not change it for anywhere in the world. People laugh and are happy, and the symbol of the town is a fat, jolly man, clearly having a good time.

Recently I went to the opening there of the Embassy Centre, a new theatre with nearly 1,200 seats, of which the lower rungs are retractable, so that a large area can quickly be cleared for wrestling, trade exhibitions, boxing, banquets and fairs. There is an excellent rake, so one does not need to dodge back and forth behind the bouffant hair of the lady in the row ahead, and there is a lot of room for knees. Have we not all suffered appalling discomfort with our kneecaps crunched into the seat in front while we tried to concentrate on the well-known aria or the deathless prose? Skegness has always specialised in summer shows, and this new seafront theatre, with its grey and red 1930s entrance, saved from the former building, with its smart new foyer and bars on two floors, one of which has a terrace with gardens leading to the sea, will attract many of the famous names in show business to entertain visitors to this welcoming town.

Further along the coast there is Batemans, the nineteenth-century family brewery where real ale is still made and bubbles in the vats, giving off that sweet, scented smell of the hops. Nowadays that is indeed rare. I used to see similar great vats in Watney's Brewery at Mortlake, but today the Carlsberg Brewery at Northampton, and Bass at Burton on Trent, are comparable to spaceships, with buttons, flashing lights, acres of chromium plate and endless complicated tubes or canisters of stainless steel, but nary a drop of beer. So much for technology, but happily beer is still a favourite English drink, and exported all over the world.

North of Skegness is Mablethorpe, a smaller seaside resort where enthusiasts for veteran cars will love the newly established car museum, started by a garage owner, and housed in a former Council Bus Station. There are most unusual cars,

Above and below right Tattershall Castle. *Below left* A notice on a tree in the Broadway

including a 1929 Citroën grape pick-up truck from France, hidden from the Germans during the war. There is a maroon Buick convertible of 1938, which belonged to Clark Gable, a BMW, and a Wolseley four-seater tourer of 1927. I was intrigued to see an Austin A40, a twin of the one I used to drive almost twenty-five years ago, when I was a voluntary Care Committee worker for the London County Council in Wandsworth and Vauxhall. My A40 used to carry me up and down Lavender Hill, where the 'Mob' came from, depicted in that droll film from Ealing Studios, and seeing the solidity of its doors and windows, the comfort of the seats and the careful finish of the bodywork, it seemed, although relatively modern, already to belong to a more leisured age.

But perhaps the most exciting attraction of all on this bracing Lincolnshire coast is the Nature Reserve at Gibraltar Point, south of Skegness, on the northern tip of the Wash. There are 1,100 acres of sand dunes, salt marshes, and the foreshore, where all kinds of flora, fauna and migrant birds can be found.

We arrived at sunset, and the streaks of pink and orange across the sky dipping into Wainfleet Haven which housed a solitary fishing boat, the uneven lines of scrubby grass which drew the eye towards the port of Boston, eighteen miles away, and the faint glimmer of water in the deserted marsh-land, contrasted with the brightly-lit Field Station with its display of dried flowers and exotic pebbles, and the enthusiasm of the young warden and his pretty wife.

This is one of the finest nature reserves in England, if not in Europe, and obviously the birds know it, because from the end of April onwards there is a regular influx of migrants – in the spring, swallows from South Africa and warblers from Italy, in the autumn, brent geese from Scandinavia and the Arctic Circle and the great grey shrike from Northern Russia. There are black-caps and white-throats, field-fares, snow-buntings and bartailed godwits. In the ponds there are moorhens, coots, mallards and tufted ducks, and birds of prey like the kestrel, and the short-eared owl, which eats the voles in the grassland.

Every year about 200,000 people, ranging from school parties to clubs of naturalists and ornithologists, come to study the habits of birds and look at the shrubs which can provide their food. In the sand dunes the bright red buckthorn berries are eaten by the birds in winter; and willowherb and lady's bedstraw grow nearby. Couchgrass, sea lavender, sea purslane and sea asters thrive on a diet of salt in the marshes, while on the foreshore cockles and lugworms are like caviar to the curlews, knots and grey plovers.

Bird-watching takes place in the early mornings, and in the Observatory experts catch and ring some of the migrants in order to study their habits, and to learn more about this phenomenon of nature, which allows birds to breed and take a holiday in a warmer climate than their own.

Lincolnshire can truly cater for all tastes; for those who want to walk alone, for those who are happiest in a crowd; for those who want to feel part of history, or for those who just want to have a rest. It can all be encompassed from the reassuring base in the pinewoods of Woodhall Spa.

BUXTON SPA

WHEN WE WENT to the Festival it was a still, sunny evening in July. We took the high road from Baslow across the plateau; the fields with their dry stone walls of Derbyshire limestone fell away on either side, and we could see for miles across to the Cheshire plain and the Staffordshire moorlands. For this is Peakland, given its name by the settlers called *Peacs*, who chose to come here even before the Romans turned Buxton into a holiday camp for their northern legions. It is the land of the Dark Peak and Kinder Scout, of Mam Tor and the Blue John mines, where water pours down the ravines and where in the cave of Beeston Tor Saxon coins and jewellery were hidden in 874 from the Danish invaders. There are miles of narrow roads which intersect this wild hilly area of gritstone and limestone, where market towns and villages are found in the shelter of the valleys.

The Spa town of Buxton, mainly the creation of the fifth Duke of Devonshire, is a sudden, stunning, Georgian surprise. You are completely unprepared for the first sight of the Crescent, built in 1784 by Carr of York, or for the dazzling view from the height of Hall Bank of the dome of the Devonshire Hospital, three inches larger than St Peter's in Rome, framed by the trees of Corbar Hill.

On the Slopes, in front of the Town Hall, Palladian vases lead the eye down to the colonnade and to the former Pump Room opposite, now the Micrarium, where all kinds of insects and small mammals can be studied beneath large illuminated microscopes.

Just around the corner is the Square. Its arcaded frontage reminds one of Venice, yet the scale is so agreeable and the elegance so understated that it is the typical English throw-away line that foreigners find hard to understand.

But the centre of life in Buxton is not the Square, nor the Crescent, nor the elegant Quadrant with its arched upper windows above the ground-floor shops, but the Pavilion. The Pavilion was built in 1871 by Milner, assistant to Joseph Paxton, the Duke's gardener at Chatsworth. It stands in twenty-three acres of gardens where beech and lime trees give shade in the summer, where there are bowls, boating, and donkey rides for the children, and where mallards and muscovy ducks disport on the River Wye which flows beneath the white-painted bridge. The Pavilion itself is like a miniature Crystal Palace, with glass walls supported by delicate spandrels of wrought iron, which in the Conservatory are painted dark green and red to complement the azaleas, banana plants and oleanders, and the miniature birds in the aviary which add an exotic flavour.

The Conservatory in the Pavilion

The youngest festival-goer   Senior citizen in Pavilion Gardens

I first entered the Octagon ballroom in winter, when the gardens outside were covered in snow, and the cold wind caused the frosted leaves of the trees outside to tap against the windows. We seemed isolated in a palace of glittering spun sugar, like Lara and Zhivago in their dacha in the Russian countryside. Yet only the previous week, music, lights and whirling froths of spangled tulle had animated the scene for the BBC programme *Come Dancing*. Parties, banquets and even an indoor circus have also been held in this unusual setting. Every day, in another part of the Pavilion, residents and visitors gather in the warm restaurant or café for lunch and relax with books or newspapers as they look out over the gardens to Grinlow Woods, while others swim in the covered pool filled with natural spring water.

During the July Festival, Buxton is *en fête*. Flags fly, the flowers are in bloom, the town is full, and the entrancing Opera House comes into its own. Frank Matcham in 1903 designed the blue-and-gold plaster-work of cupids blowing imaginary fanfares, and there was an atmosphere of excitement and anticipation when we arrived for the opening performance of the Hungarian musical fable *Háry János*. Ladies were in long summer dresses, gentlemen wore dinner jackets, and this intimate Opera House provided the perfect background for such a special outing. In the interval we strolled on the terrace where Morris dancers were in the midst of their intricate steps, while a musician attracted a small crowd as he sat on the grassy banks and played his guitar. Exhibitions, master classes, films, jazz and a toy fair, are all part of this many-sided Festival.

But if you want to see Buxton without the razzamatazz of organised entertainment, why not walk down the broad tree-lined avenues with their Italianate villas towards the smaller stone houses of Higher Buxton and Burbage Village, or wander beside the river down Serpentine Walk? If you feel really energetic, follow the steep paths up to the Cat and Fiddle, at 2,000 feet above the Goyt valley the highest public house in England, or try your skills on the Cavendish Golf Course, which has sweeping views of the Staffordshire Moorlands.

I love Cavendish Circus, in the centre of the town, with its antique shops protected by glass canopies edged with wrought iron; the post box of 1879 opposite the Opera House; the classical ceiling painted white, pink, crimson and gold in the former Crescent Assembly Rooms, now the public library; and the private houses in Burlington Road, the Park, and the Broad Walk which faces the lake of Pavilion Gardens. There seem to be trees everywhere to frame the buildings, while the sloping streets lead the eye up or down to yet another building, another architectural detail. Perhaps it is the contrast between the sophistication of the houses and the primeval aspect of Axe Edge and Dark Peak, where wallabies roam wild near Lud's chapel, which makes Buxton such an exciting town.

In the Middle Ages so many cures were attributed to the good offices of St Anne that the walls of St Anne's Well nearby were hung about with votive offerings of crutches and miniature arms and legs in gold. During the Dissolution of the Monasteries, Thomas Cromwell sent Sir William Bassett to seal up the Well and raze the chapel to the ground. An extract of his subservient letter to Cromwell reads:- 'And for that there should be no more idolatry and superstition there used, I did not only deface the tabernacles and places where they did stand, but also did take away crutches, shirts, and shifts, with wax offered, being things that allure and entice the ignorant to the said offering . . .'

It has always proved difficult to stamp out fervently-held beliefs, and for many years pilgrims continued to flock to the Well from all parts of Yorkshire and Derbyshire. Many were poor and destitute, and since the monasteries were no longer there to give them food and shelter, the residents of Fairfield, that part of Buxton where the Well was situated, sent a petition to Queen Elizabeth to complain that the money set aside for church repairs had to be spent on these poor wayfarers.

In 1573, Mary Queen of Scots, a prisoner at nearby Chatsworth, was allowed to visit Buxton to help alleviate her rheumatism. She stayed at Old Hall, where an hotel now stands, and visited the Bath House, built a few years earlier by the Earl of Shrewsbury, who had installed a fashionable doctor.

In the reign of William and Mary, the warm bath and well were at Buxton Hall, and Celia Fiennes, who made a comprehensive tour of 'Spaws' in England, stated that the lodgings were so crowded that sometimes 'three must lye in a bed'.

In the late eighteenth century, subscribers to the Buxton Ball Room included the Countess of Derby, the Duke of Manchester, the Dowager Countess Spencer and the Earl of Scarborough. Balls, which began at seven o'clock, tea-parties and card-playing were part of the entertainments, but after the Archbishop of Canterbury became a subscriber in 1789, a new rule ordered 'the Card Room to be locked up on the Sabbath Day'.

Behind the Crescent, the Great Stables were erected; they housed 300 horses, with rooms above for horsemen and grooms, and in the centre was a circular exercising court. In 1858, these former stables, converted to become the Devonshire Hospital, were presented to the town by the 6th Duke, and today treatments are still given for rheumatism on the National Health Service, and in the laboratories research continues to find some permanent cure for this painful disease.

Near to the Square is the bottling factory for Buxton Water, which sells not only in this country, but increasingly all over the world. The actual water can be seen bubbling at 81.5° Fahrenheit, and it is a thrilling sight as the large bubbles pop as they reach the surface. The heat is activated by the reaction of the water to the volcanic limestone miles below ground, and the old saying about water dripping on a stone is amply justified when you visit Poole's Cavern, where water over the centuries has formed stalactites and stalagmites and worn the rocks into curious shapes.

South-east of Buxton lies Cromford, famous not for natural phenomena, but for one of the most ingenious inventions of the Industrial Revolution, the water-powered cotton spinning mill. Sir Richard Arkwright, born in Preston, was a barber and travelling wig-maker, when his inventive mind, seeing red-hot iron drawn between rollers, adapted the idea to a spinning frame made on the same principle, so that the cleaned and carded cotton was drawn between two pairs of rollers, the second moving quicker than the first. To avoid the Lancashire machine wreckers he built a mill at Nottingham, but two years later moved to Cromford, where costs were lower and water power more easily available.

Today the mill, constructed of hand-dressed local stone, with many small windows which gave enough light on dark days to work the machinery, survives as a most interesting example of industrial architecture. Arkwright's industrial village, his water-wheel beside the pond, the Masson mills further up the river and the Greyhound Inn can still be seen as part of his grand design for Cromford, where he made roads, planted trees and started to build Willersley Castle. A boat called *John Gray* still plies back and forth along the canal built for a consortium headed by Arkwright, and the 1849 beam engines of Leawood Pumping Station, which are still in working order, can be visited in this agreeable manner.

Cromford, with all its memories of the violent changes to the economy and to the countryside wrought by the Industrial Revolution, is nevertheless a memorial to the genius of a barefoot boy from Preston who made Lancashire cotton famous throughout the world.

Only a few miles from Cromford is Holloway, where the cottages up Bracken Lane seem to cling to the hillside, while hundreds of feet below the Derwent flows beneath Lea Bridge. It was here that Florence Nightingale spent her youth, at Lea Hurst, a seventeenth-century house enlarged by her father in 1825. From the nursery windows she had an uninterrupted view across the valley to the hills opposite, and down to where the river roars over the rocks. After Scutari she returned, unannounced, alone, perhaps wishing to be soothed and refreshed by the

Cloisters in the Square

invigorating scenery of this part of Derbyshire. Below Holloway is the tiny hamlet of Whatstandwell. Stone from its quarries used to take a fortnight by canal to reach London, where it was used for the Houses of Parliament. Here and in the surrounding villages the stone is deep pink, which gives a softening effect to otherwise severe buildings.

The local market town is Wirksworth, once the centre of the lead-mining district known as the King's Field. The mines were worked by Romans and Saxons, and the Domesday Book records that the ore was also smelted in hearths in the surrounding hills. The steep streets, little alleys like Bowling Green Lane, and the eighteenth-century buildings grouped in the centre give Wirksworth a friendly atmosphere. There are old shop-fronts like Brazier and General Ironmonger, and tucked away behind the main street there is a church, started in 1272, which contains some unusual monuments. Sir Anthony Gell, of Hopton Hall, who founded the almshouses and grammar school in 1576, is carved in alabaster, with a beard and moustache, and lies on an elaborate tomb in a long gown with ruffs at his

Morris dancers at Buxton Festival

Fringe music in the open air

neck and wrists. The organist told me that every year on Founder's Day, when a special service is held, the children come to offer a wreath to their patron of long ago. On the other side of the church there is a splendid Renaissance monument to Anthony Lowe, with a brightly coloured coat of arms in which a scarlet dragon puts out its forked tongue. On the north wall there is an extremely rare Anglo-Saxon coffin lid of 800, discovered in 1820. It shows the life of Christ, and the stumpy little figures with large heads, as in a child's first drawing, enact amongst other scenes the washing of the Disciples' feet, the Crucifixion and the Presentation in the Temple. Just by the main door there is another Saxon carving of the King and Queen of Hearts; the huge heart of the Queen reaches almost to her chin, reminding one of a modern naïve painting.

From Wirksworth the road north will take you to the resort of Matlock Baths, dominated by the rocky Heights of Abraham, and on to Matlock, a former spa, where now the Hydro, with its domed winter garden high up on Smedley Street, is used as the council offices. Down the very steep hill is Hall Lees Park, with its pretty bandstand, and on the skyline the impressive ruins of Riber Castle.

But I want to take you to the south-west, to Ashbourne, where Nestlé bottle the natural water, and where in the church with its tall, slender spire are some of the most striking church monuments in Derbyshire. Sir Thomas Cockayne, who guarded Mary Queen of Scots while she was in the county, is shown life-size, kneeling, facing his wife across a prayer-desk, while below on the praedella are their ten small children. Another of the alabaster tombs shows Sir Humphrey Bradbourne, dressed in armour in preparation for the Armada, with his sixteen children carved on the sides, three who died young wrapped in swaddling clothes.

But it is the youthful Penelope Boothby who commands the attention. She lies on her side in a white marble dress tied with a sash with pinked edges, a ribbon round her hair. Her feet and arms are carved in the most meticulous detail by Thomas Banks, who showed his work at the Royal Academy Exhibition in 1793, when Queen Charlotte saw it and burst into tears. It is a poignant memorial to a little girl, and the shining white marble is in strong contrast to the Elizabethan Knights in their faded yellow alabaster. Outside, the row of fifty lime trees in the churchyard, and the Grammar School opposite of 1585 with its leaded, diamond-shaped window panes, are all features of this lovely town where Prince Charles Edward stayed at Ashbourne Hall before his ill-fated journey into Derby.

Bowls in Pavilion Gardens

It is well worth a short detour to the village of Fenny Bentley, whose small church has a carved wood screen of the early sixteenth century. Two macabre and recumbent figures, their features obscured by rigid alabaster shrouds, represent Thomas Beresford, who died in 1473, and his wife, commemorated in this weird way over a hundred years later.

But enough of gloom and death. We will go north to Bakewell, where in Ye Olde Bakewell Pudding Shoppe you can still buy one of these delicacies made from the original recipe, first served in 1859 at the Rutland Arms Hotel, and known elsewhere as Bakewell Tarts. They are composed of crisp pastry, jam and a kind of custard. I went to the town on market day, and there were stalls galore just behind the seventeenth-century market-house which is in process of restoration. There are antique shops with fine oak and walnut furniture in King Street, away from the bustle of this busy town; there are stone houses and old inns, a church in the shape of a cross and a little pack-horse bridge of 1664. The most important Agricultural Show in the North Midlands is held here in August, but people come to this attractive town at all times of the year, and in the summer it is crowded with visitors who also want to see Haddon Hall, only a few miles away.

Originally the home of the Vernons, who had possessions in Normandy, parts of this ancient manor house, which with its battlements resembles a castle, were built before 1300. The courtyard, the banqueting hall, the old kitchen, the Tudor dining-room and the long gallery are all unique in their excellent state of preservation, and the story of Dorothy Vernon of Haddon Hall, who is said to have stolen away during a ball to elope with the dashing Sir John Manners, has caught the imagination of the romantically-minded down the centuries. It is not just the overall grandeur of this house, but also the details which are so compelling. The boar's head over the lead water pipes; the way the stone slabs in everyday use for centuries are nearly worn away by footprints on either side of the aperture in the great door; the topiary peacock; the oriel window; and the heavy iron bolts which secure the entrance against intruders.

At nearby Rowsley, the Peacock Inn, with its gables and latticed windows, has since 1652 welcomed visitors as distinguished as the painter Sir Edwin Landseer and Longfellow, author of *Hiawatha*. From here the energetic can climb Peak Tor, explore Stanton Moor, with its stone circle and burial grounds of the Bronze Age, walk through Haddon Woods or fish peacefully beside the Derwent.

Further on is the little village of Beeley, with its well-kept stone cottages, the stream trickling over the rocks beside the winding road and the tiny General Stores. This brought back memories of my childhood, when two-penny worth of sweets or licorice allsorts from a huge glass jar was a special treat, and village gossip was exchanged while the price of bacon, tea and sundry other purchases were totted up on the back of an old envelope.

Alas for those children and grown-ups who have only ever known supermarket shopping, despite its undeniable advantages. That laden counter in our village shop, even in wartime, with the homely figure behind who knew exactly what went on in every house – who was ill, who was pregnant, who was currently making eyes at our bachelor vicar and which of the local poachers had been the most successful during the week – was the focus of village life, and going there was an important social occasion.

Just at the end of Beeley village a greyhound leapt over a garden wall and disappeared into a house, reminding us that coursing for hares still goes on in many parts of Derbyshire. The popular Devonshire Arms has carriage lamps on either side of the front door, and as I was peering through the windows at the snug bar and the highbacked settle by the open fireplace, I was welcomed inside and shown round by mine host who, surprisingly, came from Seville in Spain.

And so to Edensor, in Chatsworth Park, a model village where no two houses are the same, and where Joseph Paxton and John Robertson must have had the greatest fun adding a turret here, a battlement there, to their nineteenth-century houses. These are spaced well apart and dominated by the 1867 church of Sir George Gilbert Scott, who built the splendid Foreign Office in London and designed that symbol of Piccadilly Circus, the graceful statue of Eros. The Norman pillars remain in the nave and south porch, and in the Cavendish Chapel, beside a wreath of everlasting flowers from Queen Victoria, there is a white marble plaque to Lord Frederick Cavendish, who was sent to Dublin in May 1882 as Chief Secretary to the Viceroy, the 5th Earl Spencer, and only three days later at the age of 45, was stabbed to death with a surgical knife in Phoenix Park.

A few hundred yards away, as the road dips towards the river, we get our first view of the sublime Chatsworth. The deer-park designed by Capability Brown and the bridge with its three arches lead the eye towards the parterre, the fountains, the terraces, the Cascade, and to the moors beyond the wooded hillside above the house itself. Talman, Archer and Wyatville all contributed to different wings, and Paxton anticipated the wonders of his Crystal Palace of 1851 when he laid out the magnificent gardens. The first Duke sent for Tijou to fashion the exquisite wrought iron, commissioned Laguerre to depict the life of Julius Caesar in the Painted Hall and asked Samuel Watson to carve, from a design by Cibber, the reredos of alabaster for the Chapel with its columns of black Derbyshire marble.

Sir James Thornhill, whose masterpieces are the cupola of St Paul's and the Painted Hall at Greenwich, decorated the ceiling of the west stairs and the Sabine Room, and much of the grand gilded furniture is by William Kent, made for the villa of Lord Burlington at Chiswick.

If Chatsworth were in France it would without doubt be considered a Palace and treated with the awe and wonder with which tourists today approach Versailles. Situated in Germany it would be the equivalent of Herrenchiemsee, the forlorn unfinished pastiche of Versailles where King Ludwig waited in vain for his hero, Wagner, to present *Tannhäuser* in the theatre he had designed to please the composer. But it is impossible to animate the dream palaces of Ludwig, however impressive, and it needs all the wit, observation and deft descriptions of Nancy Mitford, sister of the present Duchess of Devonshire, to conjure up for us the balls

The Park at Chatsworth

and card-parties, the masques and intrigues of the courtiers in those far off days of the Sun King. In contrast Chatsworth is, with typical British understatement, a house. A house which has been altered and embellished over successive generations, and where Cavendishes have grown up in the simple nurseries. They have served their country as Ministers of the Crown, died on active service, or lived to grow old and continue to collect pictures, furniture or marbles for the Sculpture Gallery.

I have been to Chatsworth many times over the years, and it is a house for all emotions. Lovers can idle past the romantic cascade; art historians can compare the old masters to those in public galleries; people wanting a day out can picnic in the park or have tea in the stables built by Paine; others can relax and admire the *trompe-l'oeil* violin, the vast Library with its elaborate ceiling, or the white marble sculpture by Canova of Napoleon's mother, Madame Mère. It is a house that feels lived in and loved. The Duke and Duchess and their son attend to all the details which make it such a happy place, enjoyed by the hundreds of thousands who journey there each year. The Duke's study, following the tradition of his forebears, is stacked with canvases he has acquired from living artists and crammed with treasures he is collecting for this remarkable house which is still a family home.

In 1824, our ambassadress in Paris, Countess Granville, born Harriet Cavendish, wrote from France to her brother Hart: 'They asked me mints in a shop the other day for two hideous bits of the old purple Spa, set as candlesticks.' This was Blue John, from the mines still being worked at Castleton. In the eighteenth and nineteenth centuries it was highly prized when made into vases or brûle-parfums with enrichments of ormolu designed by Matthew Boulton at his Soho works in Birmingham. Sometimes it was fashioned into bowls which could be lit from inside to show off the delicate shades of colour, ranging from lilac and amethyst to yellow and amber, of this fragile Derbyshire fluorspar.

We went to Castleton by way of Peak Forest, once the hunting ground of kings and thus outside the jurisdiction of the Bishop. Runaway lovers were married here in the seventeenth-century chapel of King Charles the Martyr. Couples used to arrive at least once a week until the act of 1753 which made it illegal, but subsequent parsons continued for another fifty years to perform these illicit nuptials. Nearby, below Eldon Hill, is the so-called Bottomless Pit, one of the miracles of the Peak, into which travellers rolled stones to try and fathom the depth until the bottom was first reached at the end of the eighteenth century.

A few miles away through the mountainous scenery of Mam Tor is the capital of the High Peak, Chapel-en-le-Frith, where in the cobbled market place, raised above the main street, are the old wooden stocks in which the hands of local wrongdoers were locked while passers-by pelted them with refuse or rotten fruit and vegetables. The original church was used as a prison for 1,500 Scottish supporters of Charles I when they were routed by the Roundhead army at Preston. From the churchyard there are sweeping views of Combe Edge, Kinder Scout and Eccles Pike.

The approach to Castleton is up a winding hill. Suddenly, at the top, we saw a blaze of coloured lights which turned out to be illuminated Christmas trees, over sixty in number, outside the shops and houses. It was a wonderful welcome on a cold December afternoon, and we fell upon home-made cakes and scones in Rose Cottage, and gazed at the brightly-decorated shop windows which offer many tempting wares, including silver and gold jewellery set with the local stone.

The small museum contains a scaled-down replica of the Cavern, and the centrepiece is a circular table, mounted in ormolu, the entire top a piece of Blue John, with markings not unlike the cross-section of an old tree, but in the translucent colours of this beautiful fluorspar. From the Old Tor vein, the Blue Tor Vein, and the Twelve Vein discovered by the Romans when they established Anavio, now called Brough, only three miles away, there are numerous tazzas, columns, vases, urns and an eighteenth-century clock. Perhaps the most unusual of these treasures is a many-faceted ormolu box inlaid with panels of Blue John, recalling the jewel casket in which King Philip discovers the guilty secret of the Queen, betrayed by Princess Eboli, in Verdi's opera *Don Carlos*.

Pliny mentions in his writings that both Nero and Petronius gave high prices for Blue John vases, and in the 1750s Matthew Boulton did a brisk trade, but the first known ornamental use in England was in the music room at Kedleston, where Robert Adam decided to incorporate it into the design of the chimney piece.

I was interested to watch the working and polishing of the rough spar which has to be constantly dipped into yellow resin between each process to prevent the crystals from becoming chipped. In the actual mines at Castleton, a series of descending caverns reveal stalagmites and stalactites, shimmering crystallisations, and Lord Mulgrave's Dining Room, once a whirlpool at the meeting place of two underground rivers, where a dinner for local miners was held many years ago. In the Variegated Cavern streams run down from the roof, and throughout the mines there are fossils within this stratum of carboniferous limestone, of coral, shellfish, and the Sea Lily, absorbed into the rock when the seas were warm, shallow lagoons.

This northern part of Derbyshire is rich in great houses, and a few years ago we had a picnic amid the ruins of Sutton Scarsdale, high on the hill which overlooks the devastation of open-cast coal mining. Re-modelled by Smith of Warwick in 1724 for the 4th Earl of Scarsdale, a supporter of Charles I, today only the fluted pilasters, faint traces of the fine plasterwork by Artari, and the centre pediment on the main front, remain to remind us that once this was the grandest mansion in the county. Sacheverell Sitwell, who saw it before it collapsed, described it as 'A long, low building with a Corinthian, stone façade, of supreme elegance . . . '. His own

The Devonshire Royal Hospital

Vicar hurrying to work

St Anne's Well

family house, Renishaw, with its fine chimneypieces by Chambers, and the stucco ceiling in the ballroom with Prince of Wales feathers, contains furniture and objects collected by generations of talented Sitwells from all over Europe, including paintings by the modern artist John Piper.

Further to the east is Bolsover, once the home of William Cavendish, Duke of Newcastle, Governor and riding-master to Charles II when a boy, and a devoted adherent to the Stuart cause. In 1634 he entertained Charles I and Henrietta Maria to a feast at the Castle for which Ben Jonson wrote the masque *Love's Welcome*. The Duke's private army, the Whitecoats, fought for the King at Marston Moor, and after the Roundhead victory, when his castle was captured, he fled to the Continent, bankrupt. Today the remains of the Riding House, with its fine Italian doorway and rows of curved Dutch gables, remind one of the time when the Duke spent hours in schooling his team of Barbary horses acquired in Antwerp, in the cabriole, the *jétée*, and other figures of the *haute école*.

Not far away the Duke's grandmother, the brilliant, witty and ambitious Bess, Countess of Shrewsbury, had built Hardwick Hall, 'more glass than wall'. Today the countless windows still glitter in the clear Derbyshire light. The High Great Chamber with its plaster frieze depicting the Hunt of Diana; the Gallery, 136 feet long, hung with tapestries which tell the story of Ulysses, and used for walks on wet days; and the recurring motif of her initials on the battlements, combine to make this building not only one of the most magnificent Elizabethan houses in England, but a fitting background for a courageous and creative woman who built four houses and risked the wrath of Queen Elizabeth to marry her daughter to the grandson of Henry VII.

We have come a long way from Buxton. Yet I have not even taken you to the south-west to see the mullioned windows, the overmantel by Grinling Gibbons and the carved plaster ceilings of Sudbury. We have not been to the south-east, to see the gentle gardens of Melbourne, with their arbour of wrought iron, and the seventeenth-century lead statues. Nor to Kedleston, near Derby, where I once sat in Robert Adam's superb classical hall whose vaulted ceiling is supported by twenty alabaster columns, watching Oliver Reed and Glenda Jackson enact a dance routine for a film based on the D. H. Lawrence novel *Women in Love*. Kedleston was the birthplace of George Nathaniel, Marquess Curzon, Foreign Secretary and Viceroy of India, who achieved every goal in life except the one he valued most, that of becoming Prime Minister.

In Derbyshire you can visit so many places that are memorable, historic, and satisfying both emotionally and aesthetically. The landscape constantly changes emphasis, from the grasslands where sheep graze behind dry stone walls, to the sweeping views across the Derwent, and on to the wild expanse of moorland and rock by Mam Tor and Kinder Scout.

All this can be accomplished from the Georgian Spa of Buxton, a memorial to the 5th Duke of Devonshire, where both residents and visitors will enjoy and appreciate all it has to offer for many years to come.

ROYAL TUNBRIDGE WELLS SPA

At any time of the year it is a relaxation to stroll along the Pantiles, to see the seventeenth- and eighteenth-century houses, some weatherboarded, some with canopies supported by the original wooden pillars, to peer into the tea rooms and small shops shaded by the row of pollarded lime trees, to admire the newly-restored Musick Gallery, visited by Handel, and to linger in the garden behind the Colonnade, planted with scented tobacco flowers. In the summer a military band plays here on Sunday afternoons, and outside Binns restaurant a lantern on a wrought-iron bracket hangs over the paving.

Down a few steps is the Fishmarket, where customers of the Duke of York public house sit outside on rustic benches and watch the passers-by, or those who search for bargains among the furniture, silver and china in one of the numerous antique shops. Lanes like Pink Alley, named after a nineteenth-century mayor of the town, or Coach and Horses Passage, where once stables housed the carriages of the aristocratic visitors, lead off the Lower Walk, where tubs of geraniums and hanging baskets of flowers draw the eye beyond the wrought-iron balconies to catch fleeting glimpses of the Common.

Behind the Bath House, built in 1804, is the chalybeate spring where a dipper proffers a glass of the water. The original dipper, Mrs Humphreys, performed this task until she was 102. Nearby is the Vintry, of 1716, one of the earliest buildings in the Pantiles, with curving stone steps up to the side entrance, and opposite is Boots the chemist, who have retained their window divisions of graceful wrought iron. On the corner is a specialist shop for clocks and antique dolls, and across the road is Nevill Street, where a flat stone inserted into the pavement marks the county boundary of Kent and Sussex, in existence until 1888.

In Cumberland Walk there are many handsome Regency houses of the 1830s, some with rusticated walling and Gothic glazing-bars, one fronted with pebbles. The unusual paving here of red and greyish-blue was made at the local High Broom Brickworks. The antiquarian bookshop is a feature on the corner of Chapel Place, and one could spend hours browsing round in search of rare volumes, or rediscovering old favourites among the more popular second-hand novels and

View of the Pantiles

A house in Cumberland Walk fronted with pebbles, circa 1830

The Musick Gallery in the Pantiles

Boys playing '2-Up' in the bandstand of the Pantiles

biographies ranged outside on the pavement. There is a shop nearby which sells Tunbridge Ware, boxes or tables of inlaid lignum vitae or sycamore woods, worked into intricate patterns of cubes or mosaics and often edged with a pointed Vandyke border, much sought after in the nineteenth century. Higher up is Bedford Terrace, a row of elegant private houses with bow windows supported by brackets of wrought iron.

On the corner of Nevill Street is the Chapel of King Charles the Martyr, which opened in 1678. The uncompromising brick exterior, ornamented only by a flat weather-vane with Roman numerals and plain arched windows, gives no indication of the highly decorative plasterwork of the interior, fashioned by Henry Doogood, chief plasterer to Sir Christopher Wren. The eastern part was the work of John Wetherell, and the ceiling with its series of shallow domes, one near the organ in the form of an octagon, dated 1682, is covered with wreaths of fruit, crossed palms, husks with curled petals and winged putti. The church clock, set in a white painted turret, was donated by the actress Lavinia Fenton, who took the part of Polly Peachum in the first production of *The Beggar's Opera,* eventually married the Duke of Bolton, and settled in Tunbridge Wells.

The money to build the church was raised by public subscription from 2,400 people who patronised the spa, and the dedication was said to be a counterbalance to the Baptists and Presbyterians in the town who had called the wooded inclines above the Pantiles Mount Ephraim and Mount Sion.

The Royal Sussex Assembly Rooms

The chalybeate water was discovered in 1606 by Dudley, Lord North, great-grandfather of the Prime Minister whose intransigent policies towards the Americans provoked the War of Independence. This young nobleman, attached to the court of James I, was on his way to Eridge, hunting lodge of his friend Lord Bergavenny, hoping to recuperate from a consumptive complaint, when he observed 'ochreous scum' in a local stream, reminiscent of a similar substance at Spa in Belgium, where he had been on military service. Borrowing a bowl from a nearby cottage, he tasted the water, and brought bottles from Eridge with which to transport samples to London for analysis, where it was pronounced of medical benefit. He spread the word among his friends at court, and returned the following year. By 1608 seven new springs had been found, and people began to arrive from far and near to take the waters, some of them lodging at nearby Tonbridge, Southborough or Rusthall, before the small hamlet of Tunbridge Wells began to grow.

In 1630 Henrietta Maria camped with her entourage for six weeks on Bishop's Down, where masques and other entertainments were devised for her amusement. Another Queen, Catherine of Braganza, arrived at Mount Ephraim House in 1663, having heard that the waters engendered fertility, and it was here that Prince Rupert met Peg Hughes, the well-known actress who became his mistress and wore his gift of huge pearl drops, similar to those often seen on portraits of contemporary beauties by Lely, which had belonged to his mother, Elizabeth of Bohemia, the tragic Winter Queen.

By this time there was a Pipe-House for smoking, coffee-houses, and a walk planted with trees, where beneath the shade enterprising tradesmen displayed their wares, and local farmers offered cherries, wheat ears and quails. Plays at the Duke of York's theatre, ninepins, bowls and backgammon were other diversions, and flirtations or even sudden marriages resulted from dances and clandestine meetings. In 1698 the little Duke of Gloucester, son and heir of Princess Anne, fell and hurt himself while playing soldiers on the promenade, and his mother gave £100 for the walk to be paved. The local management took the money and did nothing, so on her return journey she installed a supervisor who arranged for the baked roofing squares called Pantiles to be laid both on the entrance square and promenade; but the Princess never returned.

Fashionable visitors continued to come to the Spa, but there was a notable lack of efficient organisation until, in 1745, Beau Nash, who had been Master of Ceremonies at Bath, arrived to impose good manners and a scale of charges, to install libraries and gaming halls, and to hire an orchestra from London which played minuets and country dances in the evening, with an interval for the drinking of tea. A print of 1748 shows the Bishop of Salisbury, Lord Harcourt, and Colley Cibber talking in the Pantiles, while Beau Nash and the Prime Minister Mr Pitt walk with the notorious Elizabeth Chudleigh, later Duchess of Kingston, who a year later attended a ball in London given by the Venetian Ambassador, naked, except for skin-tight flesh-coloured silk and one strategically placed wreath of flowers.

In later years George IV came to Tunbridge Wells and breakfasted at the High Rocks, but increasingly it was lawyers, army officers and officials from the East India Company who were deciding to settle in the town. Lord North retired here when he lost office as Prime Minister, and so did Lord Chief Justice Mansfield, who had a house on Mount Sion.

During the Napoleonic Wars, the theatre on the Lower Walk, later the Corn Exchange, was rebuilt, Regency façades gradually appeared on earlier houses, and the Royal Victoria and Sussex Hotel acquired the splendid coat of arms which is still visible today.

Decimus Burton, who designed the elegant screen and triumphal arch at Hyde Park Corner, was brought to the town by a rich merchant, John Ward, and for the next twenty years he drew up the plans for private houses and created an entirely new residential area on the Calverley Estate. Princess Victoria, with her mother the Duchess of Kent, stayed at the Calverley Hotel, rebuilt by Burton in 1840. The Crescent, with seventeen shops in its raised colonnade, was followed by Calverley Park, where Victoria Lodge, built of sandstone, leads into a group of nineteen villas with large gardens and classical details on their cornices and verandahs, which have views on to Calverley Grounds, the landscaped slope of Mount Pleasant. The concept of this estate was emulated locally in Camden Park and Nevill Park, and it was also the forerunner of planned garden cities in other parts of the country.

The area surrounding the town was always an attraction for visitors, and there is a gouache of 1753 which depicts a carriage drawn up in the courtyard of Penshurst

Place. The travellers have alighted and are being shown the house by a footman, wearing red breeches and a powdered wig. These visitors, who had been taking the waters at Tunbridge Wells, were William Pitt the Elder, the author Gilbert West and the blue-stocking Mrs Elizabeth Montagu.

We arrived at sunset, and the floodlighting had turned the stone of this crenellated fourteenth-century manor house, built by Sir John Pulteney, four times Lord Mayor of London, into a deep pink which glowed against the evening sky. The later towers, added by Sir John Devereux after the wars of Edward III, reflect the need for defences in those unstable times. The Baron's Hall, used for entertainment by a later owner, John of Lancaster, Regent for his nephew, the young Henry VI, is sixty feet high with a roof of chestnut timbers, and retains the original tiled floor on which Queen Elizabeth I danced with the Earl of Leicester. The Hall was heated by a central hearth from which smoke from the blazing logs curled upwards to a vent in the roof, and musicians played to amuse the guests in the gallery above the carved screen. From the Solar above, used in the Middle Ages as a withdrawing-room, the ladies could peer through the squint, a narrow slit in the wall, to see the activities below. Now the State Dining Room, the chairs with dark orange velvet, the oak panelling and the seventeenth-century silver wine-cooler and cistern are a foil for the family pictures in gilt frames, many on panel, including one of Lady Sidney with her six children painted in 1595, in which the eldest son, William Robert, carries a black hat with red plumes. The baby in stiff Elizabethan clothes grew up to be the father of Dorothy Sidney, Countess of Sunderland, immortalised as *Sacharissa* by the poet Edmund Waller.

The Long Gallery, panelled in pine and lit by windows on three sides, has tables of gilt gesso, a death-mask in lead of Queen Elizabeth, and a portrait of Sir Philip Sidney, with clever eyes and a sensitive face; he was a poet and scholar, and as a soldier died a hero's death at the Battle of Zutphen.

The gardens, where great arched topiary hedges are supported by the high wall of brick, were admired by John Evelyn in 1652, and the family still have the garden accounts of 1346, when teazles grew, together with fruit and vegetables.

Kent was always famous for its fruit, and by the time of the death of the first Queen Elizabeth, this county was regarded as England's main producer of apples, pears and cherries. Fruit trees were planted twenty or thirty feet apart to provide shelter for cattle or sheep, and to keep the grass damp and green during the hot summers. During the fifteenth century hops were introduced from the Low Countries, and two hundred years later one third of all the hops in England came from Kent. They were in evidence in 1600 in the village of Goudhurst, and on the outskirts today are the round oast-houses with their sloping roofs, crowned with white triangular vents, which before the nineteenth century were rectangular in shape. They have a central kiln and storage space at each end for the dried or undried hops. This pretty village has a pond with muscovy ducks, tile-hung brick

Church of King Charles the Martyr

cottages, a low-fronted hardware shop, the Church House, built in the sixteenth century, and the Burgess Stores for groceries with rows of baskets hanging outside. The sandstone church of St Mary, with its short tower of the 1630s, has a blue and gold clock with Roman numerals.

A few miles away is Finchcocks, built in 1725 of red brick, with a Tuscan doorway and an oriel window above the pediment ornamented with martial trophies. Inside there is an interesting collection of early keyboard instruments, which are played in turn by the owner to visitors who can also enjoy the concerts here during the summer months.

Nearby is the park of Scotney Castle, where sheep graze under the mature trees, and from where there are long views towards the Kent coast. In the landscaped garden, giant clumps of flowering shrubs have been planted to lead the eye down to the ruins of the old Castle, surrounded by a moat where black swans glide over the water.

We walked slowly down the paths where the tall cupressus, the rhododendrons and the variegated dogwood are planted on different levels to reveal at every turn a new vista. On the right are *Lilium giganteum*, against a background of bamboo, near the rare cut-leaf beech which stands by the stream which feeds the moat. As we stood on the wooden bridge, the sun came out and illuminated the fourteenth-century Tower with its wooded background, and on the left beyond the Victorian gabled boathouse which shelters the family boat called the *Waterlily* we could see the royal fern, the silver birch trees and the bright red berries of the crab-apple.

Spiky flax from New Zealand grows near the island on which rests a recumbent statue by Henry Moore, and near the Tudor house with its fragment of stained

In memory of King Charles

Seventeenth-century plasterwork by Henry Doogood and John Wetherell

glass bearing the arms of Henry Chichele, Archbishop of Canterbury in 1418, once owner of Scotney and founder of All Souls at Oxford, there is a stone well-head surrounded by heliotrope, herbs and pinks. On the other side of the arch on which is carved the crest of the Darell family, a lion with a long curly tail, the moat curves round a great oak tree. From the ruined entrance of the old castle one has yet another view of the walls where white wisteria blooms in the summer, and of the lime trees, azaleas and kalmias which reach up the grassy slopes of the pleasure grounds towards the Salvin house on the height above.

Bewl Bridge Reservoir, just a short distance away, has nearly 770 acres of water which is now used for fishing, canoeing and sailing. When we drove in there were countless sailing dinghies covered over with tarpaulins for protection during the winter. This reservoir, where the woods come down almost to the water's edge, and where imported shingle gives it the appearance of an inland sea, is a popular place for weekend relaxation from the spring right through to the autumn. There is riding over marked bridleways, a nature reserve, picnic areas, an adventure playground in the wood and miles of leisurely walks in the parkland.

For fishing enthusiasts, there is also trout fishing nearby in the lake of a private estate at Bayham, framed by silver birch trees, where the present house, built high on the hill in 1870, overlooks the Weald of Kent and the ruins just over the Sussex border of the ancient Abbey of the White Canons, the Premonstratensians, who were colonised from Prémontré in France.

In the sixteenth century Augustinian Monks lived at Lamberhurst Priory, where ten years ago the enterprising owner planted a vineyard for English wine on the northern slopes of this thirty-two-acre estate. There is a vineyard trail for visitors, and we saw the huge pressers where the grapes are taken when picked in October. In the cellars wine was fermenting in tanks of fibreglass or in bulbous glass carboys. At the end of the year it is filtered and prepared for bottling in February or March. It can be drunk a year afterwards, and in 1982 over 100,000 bottles of Riesling, Seyval Blanc, Reichensteiner and Müller-Thurgau were sold from this Kent vineyard.

The charm of the countryside near Tunbridge Wells is emphasized by the neighbouring villages of Bells Yew Green, with its tiny Post Office; Frant, where the Country Store is at the edge of the village green, surrounded by houses with trim gardens; and Matfield, with its Georgian houses and duckpond. But the most striking place is Groombridge. High beech hedges on the winding approach road open to reveal views of green fields and woods where bracken grows beneath the trees. At the edge of the village there is an old bridge over a stream, and the street has a sharp incline up to the cottages of The Walks, built of red and blue brick, half-hung with tiles. The sixteenth-century Crown Inn, with a large crown over the front door, the row of pollarded lime trees, and the sight of moated Groombridge Place, which lies below, with a pillared entrance, peacocks, diamond-paned windows and brick of the 1650s which has mellowed with time, and where a tiny wooden door in the side wall gives access to the water, seem part of a tale by Hans Andersen.

At Bedgebury Pinetum, open all year, a double row of pointed cypress trees curves towards the lake, where Californian redwoods, a Chilean pine of 1870 – popular in the nineteenth century for urban gardens under the name of the monkey-puzzle tree – swamp cypresses from Florida which grow in the water, and giant rhododendrons already flowering in January in this sheltered spot, make this a peaceful place for a walk. There are dwarf conifers in a special garden, and the subtle shades of green among the Bosnian pines, the Japanese silver firs and the Polish larches are highlighted by the blue of the spruce trees from the Rocky Mountains.

To the east is Sissinghurst, once the home of Harold Nicolson and Vita Sackville-West, who between them restored the house and created the garden. The low Tudor buildings of red brick, with diamond-paned windows, were built in the 1490s, and on the left-hand side there is a library, with shelves filled with 4,000 books, many of which were reviewed over the years by those distinguished writers. The medieval Persian pottery, the turquoise blue Italian glass which catches the light, the eighteenth-century mahogany rent table with its circular top of lapis lazuli and the refectory table of oak, combine to make it an entirely personal room, dominated by the portrait by de Laszlo of Vita Sackville-West wearing a large black hat and coral beads, and regarding us with intense, dark, luminous eyes, perhaps an inheritance from her Spanish grandmother, Pepita.

Her writing room was in the high tower, with its two octagonal turrets, one with a spiral staircase, from the top of which there are views for miles over the Kentish Weald and immediately below of the garden, where flowers for all seasons, colours

The Chalybeate Spring discovered by Dudley, Lord North, circa 1606

for all moods, appear in this series of outdoor rooms where herbs or roses, peonies or daffodils, are each shown in their season to the best advantage. In the white garden, the intricate box hedges first drawn to scale by Harold Nicolson on squared paper, enclose veronica, gypsophila and cineraria. In the cottage garden there are roses, dahlias and delphiniums; daffodils in the wild garden by the moat which surrounded the medieval house; and from the Rondel, where yew hedges embrace a rounded lawn, there are vistas stretching through an arch to yet another garden beyond the tower.

I loved the herb garden, and Nigel Nicolson told me that his mother used to sit there when he was a child, cover her eyes, and then without hesitation name each plant correctly as he brought her a leaf to smell. There are nearly 150 varieties, and she was always right. Today the neat notices whet the appetite for dishes in which one could include French tarragon, Corsican mint, silver thyme, chervil, cupid's dart, borage, fennel, alecost, Russian comfrey, camomile, bergamot, or Egyptian tree onion.

I remember so well as a young girl reading Vita Sackville-West's *The Dark Island*, followed by *The Edwardians*, in which the vivid descriptions of that period based on the author's upbringing at Knole bring to life the people, the parties, the clothes, the intrigues and the political undercurrents of the time, and how the house in all its unpretentious grandeur is seen in the mind's eye, so that the reality is almost like a chance encounter, after many years, of an old friend.

Today it is somehow surprising to find the entrance to Knole tucked away within the town of Sevenoaks, near to the school, with small boys hurrying across the narrow road. Inside the Park, where the dappled deer wander beside the drive, there is peace and a sense of expectancy before the house comes into view, low, grey, restrained, the second floor ornamented by curved Jacobean gables with crisp outlines, topped by the heraldic leopards of the Sackvilles. Inside the Green Court, one feels protected, part of another world, as in the courtyard of a college at Oxford, but there is still a feeling of anticipation as one advances towards the Stone Court, where the balustrade of 1748 is embellished with the emblem of the Garter, echoed on the plaques which fasten the rainwater pipes to the ragstone walls.

Inside, the staircase of 1605, carved with flowers and fruit, was one of the first to be free-standing, and the newels of leopards bearing shields, the grey and green grisaille paintings on the walls, make one want to walk slowly to enjoy every moment of the ascent to the first floor.

The Brown Gallery, with paintings of leading European figures of the day such as Sir Thomas More, Wolsey and Christopher Hatton, leads on to panelled rooms which are curiously intimate. Lady Betty Germaine's room and her china closet, with teapots of Chinese blue and white; the Spangled Bedroom where the bed is hung with dark red silk re-embroidered with ribbon; and the room of the Venetian Ambassador, with its Venetian window installed as a flattering gesture for his visit, where the four-poster bed brought from a royal palace is covered with cut velvet, with an elaborated gilded edge to the headboard and carving within the cupola.

The magnificent Ballroom, decorated by Thomas Sackville, has a deep frieze where mermaids and winged griffons are interspersed with gargoyles, and the bold strapwork on the dove-grey painted panelling is a foil for the splendour of the chimneypiece, fashioned of local Bethersden marble with reliefs of grey circles and motifs of pale apricot against a black background. In room after room there are treasures of different centuries – the Chinese burial urns, the studded armchair from Hampton Court covered with brownish-red velvet which belonged to James I, and on which he sits in the portrait at the end of the room. In the Cartoon Gallery, where each undulating panel of the ceiling contains a different design of wild flowers, the cartoons by Mytens of biblical subjects after Raphael cover the whole of one wall, and in the Reynolds room the familiar style of that artist is seen in two unusual subjects, the *Chinese page of the 3rd Duke of Dorset* and *Count Ugolini and his sons in the dungeon at Pisa.*

But nothing in the house can eclipse the impact in the King's Room of the silver furniture. Chairs, stools, mirrors, the table, the sconces and the torchères, all made in the late seventeenth century, and the sixteen-piece toilet set with scent jars, boxes and even an eye bath, make a dazzling combination. The bed hangings embroidered to match with silver and gold thread were once lined with cherry-coloured satin and surmounted by ostrich plumes in white and crimson, designed for James II at Whitehall Palace. How lucky we are to see it all.

It is strange to think that Knole, one of the great houses of England, was started in the 1450s by an Archbishop of Canterbury, when the church was all-powerful; that it survived the Dissolution of the Monasteries, and later the Civil Wars, when houses were burnt or abandoned and family loyalties often divided; that it remained through a series of different ownerships during which it was rebuilt, redecorated, embellished, used and loved, and stands today with a Sackville living within its walls, to demonstrate that individuals in each generation who aim to create beauty have a crucial part to play in the indestructible thread of English history.

The colonnade

DROITWICH SPA

ACH TIME I go to Droitwich, I marvel that this compact town can cast such a potent spell. Perhaps it is the friendly welcome; perhaps it is the profusion of black-and-white buildings of all architectural periods; perhaps it is the fact that in these days when people tend to lose their identities in the sprawling conurbations which bear no relation to the well-defined towns of the past, we feel increasingly that small is beautiful. Whatever the reason, you will love this old Worcestershire town, called by the Romans *Salinae*, the place of salt, where their military road from York converged with two others, so that the valuable commodity mined in the surrounding region could be easily transported to other Roman cities. Coins from the reigns of Claudius, Nero and Hadrian were found under the High Street, and an intricate mosaic pavement from a third-century Roman villa was discovered in 1849 in Bay's Meadow.

Today it is great fun to wander down Friar Street towards Priory House, built in 1650, which has been carefully cleaned and restored to reveal the original dark brown timber and the ornamental brickwork on the gable chimney-stacks. I remember performing the official opening ceremony a few years ago, and feeling relieved that it was in such good use. We are so lucky in this country that thanks to a strict system of Government listing, and to Council members and Council officers at all levels who have refused planning applications to demolish old buildings in their area, even when rot and decay have rendered them almost a lost cause, hundreds of thousands of buildings have been given new life and new use. I have seen comfortable flats converted from a warehouse in Lanark, and others from a prison in Bath; a university library contained in a former church at Oxford; a windmill in Norfolk used as a private house; and countless other imaginative alterations which have enabled familiar landmarks to remain as part of a town or city.

One of the most curious features of Droitwich, also in Friar Street, is the Old Cock Inn, its pointed roof topped by a cockerel, and in the upper storey a medieval window from the church of St Nicholas. After the Rebellion in 1685 of the followers of the Duke of Monmouth, natural son of Charles II, Judge Jeffreys is reputed to have held one of his infamous Assizes here, as a result of which supporters of the insurrection were sentenced to death or transported to the West Indies. One of the heads carved in stone on the outside wall, with a frog emerging from its mouth, represents the unpopular Judge. The Inn was licensed in the reign of Queen Anne, and writing over the door announces: 'Beere was first served here in the early 18th century. Ye be late.'

Almost opposite is the Norbury Theatre, built on the site of the house which was the home of Captain Norbury, a well-known naval officer, who later became British envoy to Morocco. This intimate theatre with 173 seats, which were purchased for £8 each from the old Theatre Royal, Worcester, was started in 1962 in the former dining-room of the Norbury Hotel. Now used by two amateur companies in the town, who at one time held rehearsals in the stables of an hotel nearby, they produce eight or ten shows a year. The electronic control room, the smart foyer and bar, the artistic sets designed by one of the members which would put to shame many professional productions, make this a most successful enterprise, which attracts residents of the town and people from outlying districts to programmes as varied as *Patience* by Gilbert and Sullivan, *Lord Arthur Savile's Crime* by Oscar Wilde, *Gaslight* and *Puss-in-Boots*.

Just behind the Norbury Theatre, on a higher level, is the modern shopping precinct, cleverly fitted into this older area. One wall is adorned with a glittering mosaic mural which illustrates the story of Droitwich, and shows King John in 1215 granting the burgesses of Droitwich the salt rights for which they paid £100 a year. To this day the Council depict on their coat of arms the leopards of King John, the long-handled salt barrows and the chequered top of the accounts table which in the 1350s stood in the Chequer House by the tower of St Andrew's Church.

From the earliest times salt has been an important mineral. The building of Salzburg in Austria, with its fine buildings and the magnificent Palace of the Prince-Bishop, was all financed from the revenues of the salt mines. In Droitwich, after the departure of the Romans the curiously-named Hwiccas arrived and dominated the area until ousted by King Penda of the Mercians, whose estates stretched from Bristol to the Tees and from Chester across to the North Sea. The monks were the early salt-makers, using a 'cooler', or portable barrel, and a 'loot', or rake-paddle, and by the year 836 the town had also developed into a salt-market, over which the king had rights which he could sell or assign. A hundred years later, there were at least four salt-pits, from which brine was carried to the salt-house to be cooked in the furnaces until the water evaporated, leaving behind the crystals which were loaded on to carts by Welsh slaves captured in the endless border warfare, and taken to the monastery. It was later sold in the market by the mitt – equivalent to two bushels. Local salt revenues owned by Edward the Confessor were diverted to endow Westminster Abbey, and some salt-houses nearby belonged to Lady Godiva, who once rode naked through Coventry, cloaked only in her long hair.

In 1581, 400 vats were being worked in this manner, and shares were bought and sold by investors. In 1623 a bill was filed in Chancery which suggested an improved method of using coal fires under iron boilers, but the use of wood under lead prevailed, and over subsequent years there were repeated quarrels and lawsuits

over the rights to the vats, until in 1670 Thomas Steynor broke the owner's monopoly by sinking a well on his own land and starting to manufacture the salt, causing the price to collapse from three shillings to five pence a bushel. More free enterprise followed. Sir Richard Lane, MP for Worcester, struck an underground brine river which spouted up the bore and flung workmen into the air. Salt duties were constantly evaded, and when permits to transport salt were introduced and enforced by tax-collectors, mysterious funeral processions of unknown deceased persons began to be seen continually on the move into the surrounding countryside.

In 1831, there was a serious cholera epidemic in England, for which hot baths were considered helpful. In Droitwich a sufferer was immersed in hot brine and was promptly cured. The news spread, and Dr Charles Hastings, who later founded the British Medical Association, advocated this new treatment. Existing buildings were quickly converted into hotels, a sanatorium and an assembly room. The leading entrepreneur, John Corbett, son of a canal carrier from Brierley Hill, who had developed the salt works at Stoke Prior and drastically improved the working conditions, turned St Andrew's House into an hotel and rechristened it The Raven, a play on his name, 'Corbeau', the bird which became part of his family crest. He also built the Royal Brine Baths, which were a great success, and fashionable people flocked to the town. There are contemporary paintings which show two couples in nineteenth-century clothes playing tennis outside this building, and ladies in crinolines, one leaning on two sticks, outside the Saline Baths nearby. Later photographs show a patient leaving for a drive in a bath-chair pulled by a pony, and an early touring omnibus, with raked seats and a ladder with eight steps for climbing into the vehicle, which took visitors for tenpence to see the sights of Stratford-upon-Avon. When the Salter's Hall was turned into a cinema, the talkies came to Droitwich, and one August the programme offered *Murder on the Roof*, and *The Desert Rider* – titles which could easily be given to films made today.

The High Street is still the most delightful place for a walk. There are shops selling antiques, china and curios. The gabled roofs of the timbered buildings lean over the road, some at odd angles due to subsidence from the salt workings; and on the corner is Bullock's Café, where the ancient diamond-paned windows, bordered with lead, bulge towards the sloping pavements. In 1901 this building was the Target Clothing Stores, and a photograph shows a child in a white pinafore standing against a background of straw boaters hanging outside the shop, staring at the Town Crier in his official uniform, just about to peal his bell to make an important announcement.

The Raven Hotel, where Charles II lodged in 1645 on his way to Leicester, and where Elizabethan coins were found in an oak beam in the bar, still stands in all its black-and-white splendour in St Andrew's Street. The Worcestershire, once filled with patrons of the adjacent Brine Baths, has been refurbished to cater for holiday visitors, or those who have meetings with local industrialists, engaged in ware-

The Raven Hotel

housing, cold storage, car accessories or light alloy casting, which includes the manufacture of turbine blades for the Tornado aircraft.

On the Worcester Road is the Roman Catholic Church of the Sacred Heart. It has a campanile like a church in Italy, and the interior is modelled after a Roman court of justice, with a classical altar and a lectern in white marble. The walls are entirely covered with shimmering coloured mosaics, some depicting the life of St Richard of Droitwich, who was born in 1197 to a yeoman farmer in a house on the site of the Raven Hotel. This incredibly detailed work was done between 1922 and 1932 by Gabriel Tippet from Solihull. The bright flowers and leaves, the composition of St Francis preaching to the birds in the Lady Chapel, the pillars and arches glowing with the myriad colours of the Venetian glass, create a dramatic interior. It is interesting to compare the quality and the design with the much earlier mosaics of Monreale in Sicily and with the less complete but hauntingly beautiful fragments at Ravenna.

Near the Lido, where swimmers enjoy the natural Droitwich brine, diluted to the strength of sea water, is St Peter's Fields. In the adjacent Norman church, Edward Winslow was baptised at the font surrounded with fifteenth-century tiles. Born in 1595, he was a trusted supporter of Cromwell, and left England on the *Mayflower* as one of the Pilgrim Fathers to become the first governor of Plymouth colony.

North of the Salwarpe and the Canal is Chateau Impney, now a hotel, a palace built by the French architect Tronquois for John Corbett to please his beautiful French wife, who sadly did not appreciate the exuberant architecture of brick and stone, in which there are echoes of Waddesdon and details copied from the châteaux of the Loire. It was begun in 1869, and 3,000 men worked to fashion the steep pavilion roofs, the richly decorated balconies, the ballroom with its gilded ceiling and the carved mahogany staircase which leads past stained-glass windows. From the spacious bedrooms there are wide views of the formal gardens with statues and fountains, where cupids riding on dolphins blow water from conch shells, and where once tropical trees, plants and even bananas grew in the sunken Winter Garden. From the white-painted wrought-iron bridge which crosses the lake, one can see many of the specimen trees which have grown to full maturity, and this fairy-tale house and grounds remain as a memorial to John Corbett, who restricted the use of female salters in his mines, introduced modern improvements to help all the workers, did his utmost to promote the prosperity of Droitwich and became Member of Parliament for the town, but failed to achieve personal happiness by the creation of Chateau Impney.

North-east of Droitwich is the Avoncroft Museum of Buildings. Here in the open air is a Chain Shop, where sample chains of all thicknesses hang on the outside door, ranging from those hefty enough to be anchor cables to fine chains used as part of a horse's harness. There is a forge for nails, which were hammered out to the sizes required, next to a brewhouse for washing clothes, the earliest form of laundry, where home-made beer was also brewed. The Post-Mill, where a full-time miller still grinds the corn into flour, has two sets of sails, one slatted, one of canvas,

Chateau Impney, by Auguste Tronquois, 1869

Bridge in the Park of Chateau Impney

which can be set into the wind by turning the mill, like a yacht, to extract the maximum benefit. This came from Danzey Green in Warwickshire, and although you can see part of the roof of 1320 from nearby Worcester Cathedral, many of the buildings were transported from further afield to save them from destruction.

Some of the most painstaking workmanship can be seen on Cholstrey Barn, built during the early seventeenth century. The sides are made of woven oak which looks like basketwork, and the three interior bays are formed by four pairs of curved blades which run to the roof, each pair cut from a single tree of black poplar. In the centre is the threshing-floor, where the corn in the winter months was taken from the side bays and flailed on the hard surface, and then winnowed by being tossed in a draught between the open doorways. When the building was re-erected in 1974, rafters were made by splitting the trunks of small oak trees, and the spaces between the beams were filled with oak pales woven between staves.

The Gipsy Caravan of 1890, made by Vardo of West Hartlepool, is painted bright yellow, with traditional designs, and the surprisingly spacious interior is dark red, picked out with white, lightened by engraved mirrors, and with a stove surrounded by blue and white tiles. Equally interesting is the Living Van for road-menders employed by Worcestershire County Council just before the First World War. It still contains a stove complete with old saucepans, and a sturdy oil lamp of cast iron with a coiled wick, far removed from the decorative but all-powerful lamp of Aladdin, but made in Dudley for a more mundane purpose.

The Merchant's House of 1500 from Bromsgrove with wooden shutters used when glass was still an expensive luxury; the red-brick granary; the cockfighting theatre from Bridgnorth with its triangular roof; the blue-and-white farm cart with wooden wheels banded with iron, which once belonged to Charles Martell of Laurel Farm; the nineteenth-century circular saw; and even a 1940s prefab from Birmingham, are only a few of the unusual buildings which show us how work was performed, and leisure spent, from hundreds of years ago right up to the present time.

A few miles away, set in wooded grounds in a village reached by a pack-horse bridge over the canal, is Hanbury Hall. This red-brick house with stone facings, built in 1701, is surrounded by a moat, and on either side of the entrance to the courtyard, protected by wrought-iron gates, are little gazebos with interior seats, and curious roofs fashioned to resemble Chinese pagodas, with tiles like fish scales. Inside, the eye is immediately drawn to the staircase, painted by Thornhill, which depicts Mercury almost flying across the painted cornice, about to render to the Furies a portrait of Dr Sacheverell, a Tory martyr impeached in 1710 for preaching sedition against the Whigs and the War of the Spanish Succession, which ended in the defeat by Marlborough of Louis XIV and the Treaty of Utrecht negotiated by the Tories. The other subjects represented are Thetis in Vulcan's forge, Achilles choosing a spear, Ajax and Ulysses contending for the armour of the dead Achilles, and on the ceiling the Assembly of the Gods. On the lower part of the staircase the paintings appear to be supported by a wide *trompe-l'oeil* balustrade of grisaille and gold. The dark oak staircase has exceptionally slender balusters, fluted and carved by craftsmen from Warwick.

Upstairs in the Blue Bedroom, the high four-poster bed hung with a damask of pineapple design, the deep window seats, the shutters and the slightly uneven pine panelling painted white, are in harmony with the Queen Anne walnut chairs and the Dutch marquetry commode which belonged to Lady Vernon, once owner of the house. The small bedroom has an eighteenth-century doll's house, and a lace-trimmed muslin dress for a baby hangs on one side of the cot.

In the Long Room downstairs which was once the Dining Room, there are bunches of oak leaves and Portugal laurel in bold three-dimensional plasterwork which surrounds the ceiling paintings, again by Thornhill, of the rape of Orithyia by Boreas the North Wind, and of Apollo in his sun chariot abducting a nymph. There is a large collection of Bow, Chelsea and Derby china figures of the eighteenth century, all in a remarkable state of preservation, delicate tea services from the Spode and Coalport factories, and plates filled with china flowers made at Coalbrookdale. The narrow Parlour has the original bolection moulded chimney-piece of 1700, on top of which rests Chinese export porcelain made in 1730, in a subtle shade of parchment. The curator showed me a special plate, given as a wedding present in 1728 to Bowater Vernon. In the centre is his crest, a girl holding a wheatsheaf, and on the rim, his wife's crest of three small birds. The ivory-coloured china is decorated in burnt orange, dark blue and gold, and has an almost transparent fragility. It seems incredible that so much Chinese export porcelain should have travelled half across the world and managed to remain unbroken, despite careless washing, even if seldom used, in many family collections.

The handsome Orangery, where orange trees grow in Versailles tubs, the Ice House and the Long Gallery for games, are all carefully looked after by the National Trust, who are responsible for houses, gardens and thousands of acres of hills or coastline all over Great Britain, and whose staff and voluntary helpers work unceasingly not only to safeguard our heritage, but always to show it to advantage.

Richard, Duke of York, father of Edward IV, was Lord of the Manor of Bewdley, and set up a market and a yearly wool fair in what is today one of the loveliest Georgian towns in Worcestershire. North-west of Droitwich, Bewdley was the birthplace of Stanley Baldwin, Prime Minister of England and later Earl Baldwin of Bewdley, who was fiercely proud of his Worcestershire origins. The town is set in wooded country, where the red marl in the soil is clearly visible, and where on the road from Great Witley timbered farmhouses, painted black and white, reach to the outskirts of the town. The Sayers Almshouses, founded in 1763, lead on to the handsome Georgian red-brick house, with a carved portico over the door, which belonged to the Baldwin family. The Pack Horses public house is painted blue and white, the school has a Gothic doorway, the gables of the medieval cottages have protruding eaves which hang over the road, and behind the main street are alleys and courts where small houses are tucked out of sight. We stopped in the

Nightingale Café, where there was a choice of seventeen different flavours of tea, and we ate delicious tea bread with currants while listening to a record of the *Preislied* from *Die Meistersinger von Nürnberg*.

Beyond Load Street the bridge over the river, with its three graceful arches, is by Telford, whose warehouses at St Katharine Dock in London are still visited by students of architecture from all over the world, and the former Merchants' houses on Severnside have steps up to their high front doors to obviate the danger of flooding.

Prince Arthur, son of Henry VII, lived for a short period at Tickenhill Manor, and he was married here by proxy in 1499 to Catherine of Aragon. When he died at Ludlow Castle, his bride became the wife of his brother, later Henry VIII, whose daughters, Mary and Elizabeth, both came to this Tudor house. The fifteenth-century timbers are still visible in the Great Hall, but the main rooms were modernised in the eighteenth century.

The small shops and the endless variety of Georgian houses, sometimes side by side with earlier timbered buildings, result in a townscape which is soothing to the eye, yet never dull.

The privately-owned Severn Valley Railway operates regular services from here to Bridgnorth, fourteen miles away, using renovated steam engines from the Great Western Railway, and attracts both tourists and business people.

From Droitwich there are interesting sights in every direction. The houses in the village of Chaddesley Corbett range from Tudor to Georgian Gothic, and the church has a fourteenth-century chancel. Just over the Herefordshire border, at Cleobury Mortimer, Mawley Hall, built by Francis Smith, has bold plasterwork in the hall fashioned by Artari, and there are rare woods inlaid into the walls of the drawing room with the care and craftsmanship usually applied only to fine furniture.

Patients who benefited from the Brine Baths used to refer to 'Dear Little Droitwich', and this tiny historic town, where Brine Baths will soon be operative once again, has survived many turbulent decades to remain a thriving and memorable town of the twentieth century.

Cupid on a Chateau Impney fountain

STRATHPEFFER SPA

THE FIRST TIME I saw Strathpeffer was from a helicopter. It was a clear, sunny day in May, and we flew from Inverness up to the top of snow-capped Ben Wyvis. There before us was a panorama of the Highlands, of woods and valleys, mountains and rivers, falls and streams, crofts and castles, which over the centuries have been a background for the battles, the ambitions, the dreams and the disappointments of the Scottish people.

Strathpeffer, where the neat, spotless, pretty gabled houses, with window frames and front doors painted blue, red or green, cling to the hillside framed by trees and shrubs, looks like an illustration to a fairy-tale. Goldilocks or Red Riding Hood may be just about to use the door knockers of gleaming brass, or Beatrix Potter's greedy mouse Hunca-Munca may already be inside, trying to carve the plaster chicken and angrily smashing the china fruit. But in fact the down-to-earth inhabitants are called Ross, Fraser or Mackenzie, and sell fishing tackle or sturdy hand-knitted stockings for stalking on the hills, or provide lodgings with porridge and finnan haddock for breakfast for visitors from the south.

The first thing which will amaze you is the crystal-clear air. Each breath seems to expand your lungs more fully than ever before, and a walk round this tiny spa will drive out of your system the accumulated poisons of years of urban pollution.

If you arrive by car from Inverness, you pass through Dingwall, birthplace of Macbeth, now a thriving market for sheep and cattle, and a regional centre for the police, the Council and other authorities, where equipment is made for the oil-rigs of Aberdeen. At the edge of Strathpeffer is the former station, with a notice saying 'All change for the Highlands', where sheepskins, woven leather and inlaid marquetry are offered for sale in the craft shops. The platform, where benches are set against dark red woodwork, is a relaxing place to sit and admire the white-painted wrought iron which supports the glass canopy, the roses planted where once porters would have left their barrows, and the belt of trees on the hills beyond the track. Nearby is the Edwardian villa of Timoru, built of local stone, with balconies on the first floor overhung by gables painted pale blue and white which are supported by slender columns linked by graceful arches. The Strathpeffer Hotel, hung with baskets of flowers, is painted black and white, and the many private houses have roofs of Ballachulish slate. Some have walls of Canadian red cedar, others are of pink sandstone from the nearby coast.

The Shieling once sheltered the entrance to a subterranean reservoir, and now

The station

has a tempting display of mufflers or Scottish tweed, and in the adjacent square, next to the Spa Pharmacy, Mrs Fraser's Shop sells tartan rugs, plaid skirts and tam-o'-shanters. Opposite, up a grassy slope, is the tiny Victorian building, painted bright emerald green, which is the Bank of Scotland. It reminded me of Jimmy Muir, a friend who was kind to us when we were evacuated to Canada in the war, who had left Glasgow as a young man with ten shillings in his pocket, and ended his career in Montreal as President of the Bank of Canada.

Further along is Spa cottage, a boutique called the Spa Spot, and above on an incline the Highland Hotel of 1900, which has a tartan stair-carpet. From its carved wooden balcony you can see the houses and cottages with their trim gardens, surrounded with trees, which are built in layers towards the summit of the hills, beyond which is the challenging golf course with views towards Cromarty Firth and the mountains of Wester Ross.

There are wrought-iron thistles on the gates leading to the Pump Room, built of pink sandstone, which still dispenses spa water in the tiled interior, and where from the end of the seventeenth century sufferers drank the sulphur and chalybeate waters to cure 'swellings, ulcers and Scorbutic or other disorders of the blood'. In 1777, the Minister of the parish recorded that William Smith, Master of Fortrose Grammar School, and Angus Sutherland of Kincardine were so lame and feeble that they were carried to the Well on carts padded with feather mattresses, but after a few weeks of drinking the waters they recovered completely and were able to walk for miles. The Minister tried to persuade the Area Commissioners to erect a good 'House, kitchen, and stable upon the Farm of Kinettas, near the goat pasture', but it was not until 1819 that a forty-foot long wooden pump room was built, and a regular service established. Visitors were charged two shillings a week, but poor people paid nothing at all.

In 1871 the Countess of Cromartie, Mistress of the Robes to Queen Victoria, and married to a local landowner, built a stone Pump Room and other buildings including the Pavilion, used for concerts, and surrounded by gardens for bowls, tennis, and croquet. She had travelled to several continental spas, and insisted that the architecture of the rest of the town should be interesting and original. Designers were commissioned from London and the locality, and the clever arrangement of the houses, which still delights us today, was the imaginative planning of Anne Cromartie, backed by private investors and the Cromartie Estate. Her second husband, Colonel Blunt-Mackenzie, erected a power plant in Glensgiach in the 1890s to supply electricity to Castle Leod, and it was soon enlarged to provide light and power for the town and for the cottages on the Heights, many years before other areas in the Highlands had such modern amenities.

Visitors to the spa used the two-horse coaches, costing ten shillings inside, six shillings outside, which took three hours to reach Inverness. Nowadays it is only a twenty-minute journey, since the opening in 1982 by Queen Elizabeth the Queen Mother of the Kessock Suspension Bridge over Moray Firth, linking the Black Isle with Inverness.

A branch line railway opened in 1885, resulting in a new influx of travellers, who in the peak of the season used the sleepers direct from London. Brakes and cabs took these passengers to their hotels, while the commuters of those days, solicitors and businessmen who worked in Dingwall and nearby towns, replaced them in the first-class compartments, and clerks, shop assistants and school children crowded into the less expensive carriages.

At seven o'clock each morning Sandy the Piper woke the patients with the plaintive but inexorable music of the pipes, and from seven-thirty onwards the hot waters were imbibed, and sufferers endured baths of diluted sulphur and massage under a spray of heated water. A variation on the continental mud bath was the peat bath. Patients were lowered by straps into what appeared to be a black morass, and were afterwards hosed down by an attendant. After a short rest, a

Timoru (*above left*) and other houses in the village

Swedish masseur would arrive to improve the circulation by vigorous pummelling, and this entire process cost about ten shillings.

Playing golf, walking, and watching Ross County play Edinburgh Wanderers on the cricket ground of Castle Leod, surrounded by trees, were other relaxations. The band in the Gardens, evening concerts in the Pavilion, or the magic lantern show by Ernest Shackleton of his travels in the Antarctic entertained guests such as the Duke and Duchess of Teck, parents of Queen Mary, Robert Louis Stevenson, George Bernard Shaw and Mrs Pankhurst, who, making a speech to a supposedly genteel gathering on the contentious subject of the equality of the sexes, was heckled and berated until pandemonium ensued.

Fishwives from the seaboard of Easter Ross also used to arrive off the train, wound about with shawls and bearing on their backs large black creels. They would offer the fish from house to house, pronounce a blessing on the family and retire into the kitchen to gut the purchases. They were given tea and food in different households, and having emptied their creels, they would refill them with articles bought for friends or neighbours before catching the train to Fearn, from which station they walked five miles to reach their homes.

In the winter, when the fashionable visitors had departed, young men and boys tried their hand at curling on Jubilee Pond, while the girls skated, or held picnics on the Island, and younger children went sledging down Main Road and Station Brae on a 'bogie' made of four pieces of wood and a cord, costing half-a-crown from the local carpenter.

Today this entrancing town, where the Episcopalian Church of pink sandstone reminds us of the strict upbringing and strong, resilient character of many famous Scotsmen, is the gateway to places which are grim or happy, interesting or spectacular, throughout the Scottish Highlands.

One day we set off for the West Coast. On the way we saw the Falls of Rogie, where salmon leap out of the water on their way upstream, and at one point the road passes beside Loch Maree, where the brooding Torridon Hills, covered with purple heather, conjure up a vision of the Scotland where men settled at the end of the Ice Age, and sheltered in the caves of Inchnadamph.

On the shores of Loch Ewe, in the path of the Gulf Stream which flows north from the Gulf of Mexico, is the garden of Inverewe. In 1862 this estate was bought by Osgood Mackenzie, who planted Corsican pine and Scots fir as a windbreak, moved rocks, heather and crowberry, and replaced the acid black peat with more fertile soil carried to the garden in creels. He put up a fence to protect plants from deer and rabbits, and started to plant rhododendrons, larch, birch, mountain ash and beech trees among the slabs of red Torridonian sandstone which is the basis of this peninsula. The dwarf *Pinus montana* was in the vanguard of trees which received the full force of the squalls from the Atlantic, and served to shelter less hardy plants, but on a fine day in September, when we wandered along paths bordered by

The Shieling

the African wand flower, lilies from Tasmania, azaleas, lobelia and the threepenny bit rose from North-West China, all was calm and serene, and the benches on the smooth lawns in front of the luxuriant herbaceous border were an invitation to visitors to sit and admire the view over the water of the mountains of Beinn Airigh Charr. The Rock garden, Coronation Knoll, The Peat Banks and Pender's Walk hold some of the 2,500 species, many of them exotic plants of vibrant colours, which in this magnificent setting grow triumphantly against all the odds.

The determination and optimism of Osgood Mackenzie reminded me of another Scot, Neil McEacharn, who decided to create one of the best botanical gardens in the world from an untidy wooded area on the northern slopes of the promontory of Castagnola in Italy. Nowadays the Villa Taranto on Lake Maggiore is visited by scientists and botanists from many countries, and the Camellia Avenue, the Lotus Lily Pond, the belt of Japanese cherries, the glade of tree ferns and the octagonal chapel with the owner's mausoleum, all meticulously cared for by the Italian state, are a lasting tribute to a successful businessman who left behind him a series of formal gardens imposed on to an Italian landscape, with the clear vision, combined with a romantic imagination, of a Scotsman who was a member of the Royal Company of Archers and a Linnaean Academician.

Higher up on the west coast, past the southern shore of Little Loch Broom, where water tumbles down the hillside into the ravines below, is Ullapool. A fishing village established in 1788 by the British Fisheries Association, it is a magnet for visitors who enjoy trout or sea fishing, bathing in the warm weather, or trips by motor-boat to the Summer Isles of Tanera Beg and Tanera Mor.

Our first view, almost from the end of Loch Broom, was of the factory ships from the Eastern bloc anchored in the bay. Known locally as Klondykers, after the adventurers who took advantage of the Gold Rush in America, these ships from Russia, Poland and Hungary remain in the harbour for months on end, and are away for years from their home base. The fish is taken direct to them by the trawlers, then processed and frozen by the specially designed equipment in the hold of the ship.

When we arrived, all was activity and bustle, with fishermen unloading their catch of herring, cod or mackerel, not on to the factory ships, but into square crates which were automatically lifted up and emptied into giant container lorries from Holland, England or Scandinavia. It seems a paradox that East and West hold such widely divergent views on the control of arms, nuclear warfare and the general conduct of world affairs, resulting in at best an uneasy relationship, yet both are obliged to seek their food, essential to the well-being of their countrymen, from the depths of the North Atlantic.

Along the front there is a strong smell of fish; seagulls whirl above the dinghies and over the Ferry Boat Inn; the Highland Home Industries sell hand-knitted scarves and berets in a cottage set back from the road up a long flight of steps, and small white-washed houses are built along the edge of the promontory. We had our picnic lunch on the beach at the end of the peninsula, where hills rise on either side,

Mrs Fraser's shop in the square

where there are views right along the Loch into Annat Bay, and where sportsmen embark on the three-hour journey over the water to the Outer Hebrides to fish for salmon and trout in the rivers and streams near Stornoway.

One evening we went from Strathpeffer to the Eden Court Theatre at Inverness to see a production by the Royal Shakespeare Company. This cleverly-designed building has a comfortable auditorium, a spacious bar, a gallery on the first floor for hanging pictures and staging exhibitions, and an excellent restaurant, out of whose angled windows there are floodlit views across the river of the red sandstone Inverness Castle.

Another day we went to Beauly, where in the main street the neat, low-built stone houses have inviting shops on the ground floor with signs proclaiming the owners to be Macrae, Fraser, Matheson, Cameron or Mackenzie, the opposite to anonymous hypermarkets or stores in countless high streets which, although trading under well-known pseudonyms, are in fact part of large conglomerates. The modern Highland Craftpoint, just outside the town, is landscaped with beds of purple and white heather, an extensive rock garden and low-level bollard lighting.

To the east is Culloden, where in April 1746 the hopes of the Gaelic people of reinstating their Stuart King were destroyed in one of the most shameful battles of

Above Ullapool. *Below* Fishing boats in the harbour

Cruises from Ullapool

history. This gaunt, windswept field has an atmosphere of defeat and death. It easily conjures up the figure of John Mor M'Gillvray, who slew twelve men with his broadsword before the pikemen killed him; or of the wounded Golice MacBane, who backed on to a wall of turf and accounted for thirteen dragoons before they cut him down. There was the impetuous bravery of Clan Mackintosh who anticipated orders, led the right of the Jacobite line against odds of two to one and shattered the first rank of the Hanoverians, only to succumb to bullets fired from the second row. The hungry, exhausted clansmen under the command of Prince Charles Edward, in his short tartan coat and cockaded bonnet, were short of a contingent, which was with Lord Cromartie in Sutherland, and without the MacPhersons and the Grants of Glenmoriston who did not receive the summons in time; but the Frasers, Camerons, Macleods, Seaforths, Farquharsons, Chisholms, Stewarts, the Atholl Brigade and the Clan Chattan Regiment were backed up by thirteen assorted guns placed in three batteries of the front line. Next were the lowland regiments, with Scottish and Irish units from the French service, and the unfit horses of the Jacobite cavalry brought up the rear. The rain and sleet blew into their faces and made it difficult to keep the powder dry; when the Hanoverian artillery opened fire they quickly put the Jacobite guns out of action.

In this battle, which only lasted forty minutes, the uncoordinated but ferocious charge of the Highlanders broke the order of the English Regiments and pushed

The Kyle of Lochalsh

Opposite above Eilean Donan Castle on the road to Skye

back the foot-soldiers, but could not prevail against Onslow's Regiment and the fire from the second line. The battalion of Lord Lewis Gordon and Drummond's Royal Ecossais advanced to give support, but already the front ranks were in retreat, leaving dead comrades lying three or four deep on the battlefield.

Men who fled to Inverness were cut down by pursuing dragoons, together with some innocent bystanders, and no quarter was given to the Jacobite wounded, who were stabbed and mutilated by Cumberland's troops. Search parties took wounded soldiers and officers from neighbouring houses to be shot, and others were chased out of turf bothies or burnt to death when troops set fire to the barn in which they had taken refuge.

Old Leasach Cottage, which survived the battle, remains today as a tiny museum where the fated day is recalled by the marble-sized bullets which were fired from the Hanoverian Brown Bess muskets; by the cruel bayonets of the 1730s; by the cannon balls which had a range of two thousand yards; and by the sword with a basket hilt which belonged to Lord Lewis Gordon, whose name is stamped on the cracked leather scabbard.

Not far from Nairn is Cawdor, approached by a bridge over a stream, where there are red and yellow lobelia in the walled garden, scarlet benches painted to match, old casks for litter and laden fruit trees, in contrast to the fortified walls and drawbridge of this turreted castle with its fourteenth-century tower.

Inside, a slender hawthorn tree of 1372 in the dungeon gives credence to the legend that, in a dream, a former Thane of Cawdor was instructed to let a donkey laden with gold choose the site for his new house. The animal lay down beneath the tree, around which the Thane constructed the vault of his tower. Upstairs is the light and comfortable Drawing-Room, with an eighteenth-century portrait of Lord Cawdor wearing a coat lined with fur, and the Family Bedroom, with its tapestries and gilded Venetian four-poster bed. The bold Jacobean cornice in the Yellow

Gardens at Cawdor Castle

Sitting-Room, the immaculate new kitchen, and the luxurious public tea-room with
friendly staff, home-made cakes, chintz curtains, a display of fine china and a large
framed panel of colourful embroidery, make this privately-owned castle a joy to
visit.

To the south we went to Blair Atholl, framed by a double avenue of limes. This is
a ducal seat with crow-stepped gables and corbelled turrets with roofs of dark slate.
The eighteenth-century State Rooms contain gilded furniture and portraits by
Ramsay, Raeburn and Lawrence, and visitors can wander round no less than
thirty-two rooms.

We went to Scone Palace, from which the famous stone is traditionally used for
each Coronation in Westminster Abbey, and where the rare ivories, the porcelain
from Meissen and Sèvres, and the unique collection of Vernis Martin of the 1830s
are rivalled only by the exquisite eighteenth-century French furniture made for
Marie-Antoinette. The table by Riesener, inlaid with olive, holly and satinwoods,
the secrétaire stamped by Nicholas Petit, the *table à méchanisme* by Topino, and the
fauteuils by Bara, covered in tapestry which depicts mythological subjects, were all
brought back to Scotland by the 2nd Earl of Mansfield, Ambassador to Paris and
Vienna.

Back to the north again is Dunrobin, whose castle with its slender turrets stands above formal terraced gardens with fountains, overlooking the sea, where in caves by the coast rock pigeons come in to roost. In the Library lined with sycamore, the de Laszlo portrait of Duchess Eileen shows her with a background of the wild moors of Sutherland. The bed used by Queen Victoria has flying doves on the four gilded posts, while in the vast Drawing-Room, whose plaster ceiling has a recurring design of the family armorials, pictures by Canaletto depict the Doge's Palace in Venice, against warm Italian skies.

Our last visit was to the haunting Isles of Skye, where the sandy beaches, the jagged peaks of the Cuillin mountains, the ruined crofts, the peat bogs and the wild, treacherous rocks evoke the period of the Palaeolithic culture, followed by the Neolithic, when short, dark people from the Rhineland found their way here to erect great stone monuments like the Ring of Brodgar in the Orkneys. Skye was drawn on Ptolemy's map of the second century, and in the ninth century Norsemen controlled both the Northern and these Southern Isles of Scotland. Once buried under the Cambrian seas, where shellfish and sea worms flourished and sponges grew, the sea beds were formed of limestone, sandstone and shale, which over the centuries emerged as the waters receded, while pollen grains and leaves trapped in the flows of volcanic lava became conifers and cedars which grew on the hill slopes, and in the bogs were water-lilies.

The coast-line of Skye today, with its tiered escarpments cut in the ancient lava, and its deep indented sea-lochs; the melancholy heath, covered with bracken and bog-myrtle; the fertile lowlands with birches and wild flowers; create a landscape which echoes the conflicting character of the Scots, with their fierce loyalties, their inventive minds, their adventurous outlook, their long memories and their infinite capacity for survival.

It was in Portree Bay that King Haakon Haakonsson anchored in 1263 en route to Largs, and in 1540 came the well-appointed fleet of James v. Dr Johnson and Boswell travelled to the island in the eighteenth century, admired the spectacular scenery, saw the ship in the harbour about to take emigrants to America, and noted the scarcity of ready money. Sir Walter Scott praised the landscape in *The Lord of the Isles*, and on Fingal's Seat, which overlooks the bay, the third-century King of Morven sat to watch his dogs hunt deer in the glen below.

But there is no episode in history which so tears the heart, and tortures the emotions, as the flight after Culloden of Charles Edward Stuart, who for five nerve-wracking months managed to evade his pursuers and find refuge on this island. Finally, he left Flora MacDonald at the tavern in Portree, and after several narrow escapes on the mainland embarked at Loch nan Uamh on the French ship *L'Heureux*, which on 19 September 1746 set sail for France.

Since that time, many other Scotsmen have left their native land to seek their fortunes on the other side of the globe. They always carry with them, not just memories, but the strength and the spirit of this gallant country, which will continue to influence men and women for many years to come.

The Turkish Baths

HARROGATE SPA

MANY YEARS AGO, I went to Harrogate to open the Northern Antique Dealers' Fair. The town was full, and as we drove in on the road from Leeds, I was conscious of a feeling of excitement, that whatever lay in store it was going to be fun. And so it was. When I returned recently, at 10 a.m. in Parliament Street cars were competing to get into town, and Betty's, the meeting place for 'le tout Harrogate', was packed to bursting with clients sampling coffee and pastries amid the potted palms. Harrogate is the place where Turkish Baths can be enjoyed in rooms decorated with saffron and turquoise tiles, where motifs of 1897 are stencilled on the oriental arches surmounted by crescents, where you change in a cabin made of solid mahogany and where handrails are made of polished brass. You can relax afterwards in the Royal Baths café and listen to the pianist who has played there for thirty years, while you gaze at the curvaceous ladies of the French faïence centrepiece filled with plants, at the old sample bottles of Harrogate water in their carved case, or admire the elaborate coat of arms over the architrave of the entrance.

Opposite are the handsome Municipal Buildings, built in 1931, and just round the corner are jewellers, silversmiths, and shops for fine antique furniture, with restrained window-displays behind the Edwardian façades. Further along, you can see the guest-houses in Otley Road, the little footpath called Byron Walk, and the solid, comfortable buildings of Yorkshire sandstone, formerly the homes of mill-owners of Leeds and Bradford in the nineteenth century, which stand in the Oval and Trinity Road, where crocuses and daffodils bloom in the spring, giving an impression of strength and permanence to this thriving town. For thriving it is, and the 500 conferences held here each year, the exhibitions which take place in one of the six halls, and the visitors who pour in from the region or further afield for shopping, meetings or holidays all bear witness to Harrogate's success.

The new conference centre which was opened in 1982 cost £28 million. Two thousand people can sit in the semi-circular auditorium, where the seats, with plenty of leg-room, are upholstered in grey and maroon tweed, as a foil to the dark maroon walls. There is every sort of modern lighting, and a stage that can activate all kinds of transformation scenes, even to complicate the arrival of the Demon King. From the cleverly-designed cantilevered interior walkway leading from the foyer to the upper floors, there are views of the older gabled houses of Harrogate through the curved glass walls. One of the first achievements of the organisers was

Staircase in the Royal Baths

to attract the Eurovision Song Contest, and they already have bookings for the Centre as diverse as product launches, snooker and the Hallé Orchestra.

I have been to several large trade exhibitions in Harrogate, and despite the series of halls and the apparently endless amount of space, some exhibitors still show their wares in different hotels round the town, and this makes one feel that the town is sharing in all the activities, and that customers are not, as in some other cities, confined to a dreary hall built in prison architecture style on the edge of a motorway, where they are almost in quarantine, well away from local people, shops, or the cheerful hubbub of daily life.

The fortunes of Harrogate were founded as long ago as 1571, when William Slingsby, riding one day over marshy ground in the royal hunting forest of Knaresborough, discovered the Tewit Well. This was the first of over 100 medicinal springs, and before the end of the sixteenth centry the chalybeate water, which purged the blood of 'cholericke, phlegmaticke, and melancholicke humours', was known to the medical profession in Yorkshire. Among those who patronised the spa in 1632 were the Duchess of Buckingham, Lady Vavasour, and the wife of the Lord Mayor of York, but they lodged in the more salubrious town of Knaresborough. Lord Morley, wishing to improve his spleen, and misjudging the political situation, was caught in 1644 by Parliamentary troops and became an unwilling lodger in Knaresborough Castle.

The earliest recorded inn at Harrogate was the Queen's Head, built in 1687, followed by the Dragon, later owned by Thomas Frith, father of the Victorian artist, and the Granby, where after the Napoleonic Wars weekly balls were held during the season to amuse visitors. Earlier, in 1769, the barn behind the Granby, converted into Harrogate's first theatre, offered David Garrick's comedy *The Clandestine Marriage*, followed by a farce, *The Virgin Unmasked*. The New Theatre, in

Church Square, attracted audiences from 1788 with comedies such as *The Fashionable Lover*, and some plays were sponsored by prominent local families. A year later, Mrs Jordan, mistress of the Duke of Clarence, later King William IV, was persuaded to play for four nights in Harrogate, 'to diversify the amusement of the devotees to sulphurated springs'.

Racing and excursions to Harewood, Fountains Abbey or Newby Hall were other diversions, and at the end of their holiday visitors felt better, not only from drinking the waters, but from the 'bracing, exhilarating air'.

In 1835 the Montpellier Baths were built, where in the Central Hall customers were entertained every morning by musicians, and in the same year the Royal Promenade Pump Room, with its classical portico, became available for concerts and dances, and also housed a subscription library. Just behind, six acres were laid out as pleasure grounds with a lake for boating, and in fine weather a band played on the terrace. Successful manufacturers from Leeds, Sheffield and Manchester began to bring their families to take the waters, besides Members of Parliament, baronets and ladies of quality.

In the last quarter of the nineteenth century several hydros were established, a skating rink was added to the Montpellier complex and the Valley Gardens were laid out in time for Queen Victoria's Jubilee. At the Spa Room visitors could see Blondin the rope-walker, balloon ascents, fireworks, and the Carl Rosa Company in the garden scene from Gounod's *Faust*. A disgruntled resident wrote to the local paper complaining of 'trashy and disgusting comic songs', but at the Town Hall the

The International Conference Centre

Above The Old Magnesia Well in the Valley Gardens.

Opposite The Museum

light operas of Gilbert and Sullivan were a great success, and Lily Langtry, dressed by Worth of Paris, once an assistant at Swan and Edgar, brought her own company to play *Peril*.

Nineteenth-century Harrogate was the creation of both public and private enterprise, and five of the first seven mayors were builders by trade. But the principle of *'rus in urbe'* has always been respected, and new arrivals are still amazed by the open grassland of 200 acres called the Stray, protected in 1770 by Act of Parliament, where oxen were roasted to celebrate Queen Victoria's Jubilee, which brings the countryside right into the centre of the town. Flowers are everywhere – on the first roundabout in West Park, which was the old turnpike crossroads near Prince of Wales Mansions, originally Hattersleys Hotel; in the Valley Gardens where bands play in the summer near the old Magnesia Well; in Montpellier Gardens; and in Crescent Gardens, which has won national and international prizes for floral displays.

The Royal Hall, built in 1903 by R. J. Beale and Frank Matcham, who also designed the Opera House in Buxton, is a theatre in the grand tradition, with red plush, gilt angels, and that indefinable atmosphere which makes you feel at once that you will enjoy the performance. It was once called the Kursaal, and great artists such as Kreisler, Paderewski, and Sarah Bernhardt in *La Dame aux Camélias* performed here before the Great War. There is a nostalgic photograph which shows a mixture of early cars and horse-drawn carriages bringing patrons to the theatre, while boys with Eton collars, a girl in a sailor suit, and fashionable ladies with long dresses and sunshades arrive on foot. The tree-lined road sweeps up past the Royal Baths to Parliament Street, where awnings or glass canopies supported by

wrought-iron pillars can be seen over the shops, which today are still some of the smartest in Harrogate, selling dresses and furs. The road then curves to the right where, just out of sight is a meeting-place for theatre-goers before a performance – Betty's.

My husband and I have been to tea-rooms all over the world, and can debate the merits of Sacher's or the Imperial in Vienna, Rumpelmayer's in Paris, Cova in Milan, or the unspeakable joy of the Café Luitpold in Munich, where in winter one takes refuge from the crisp, delicious, freezing air at five o'clock in the afternoon, walks past the mouth-watering array of their famous chocolate truffles, and orders a *Wienerschnitzel* with a mixed damp salad impregnated with their secret white dressing. We have been to hundreds of others in places as diverse as Hamburg, Cairo, New York, Baden-Baden or Budapest, but we both agree that Harrogate has one of the best of all.

Betty's was started by a Swiss confectioner in 1919 who aimed to settle in Hampshire, but somehow ended up in Harrogate. You go in past the display of patisseries made in their own bakery including Old Peculiar fruit cake flavoured with Yorkshire ale, jars of home-made marmalade and jams, down a few steps, and there is the light and pretty room, with a pianist to soothe any jangled nerves, and neat waitresses in white lace caps threaded with black velvet ribbon, and aprons edged with broderie anglaise over their trim black skirts. There are local specialities like Brontë Fruit Cake with Wensleydale cheese, or Yorkshire curd tarts with cream, and to taste these delicacies while you look out beyond the glass canopy where there are always hanging baskets of bright flowers, across one side of the green Stray, makes you feel that it is wonderful to be alive.

Your strength revived, you can be tempted by the boutiques in James Street, or the covered shops in Lowther Arcade, or by the antique furniture and china which were a magnet to Queen Mary on her frequent sorties to Harrogate whilst staying at Harewood House with her daughter, the Princess Royal.

Biscuits at Betty's

A child in the Valley Gardens

The Art Nouveau Harrogate Theatre, with its brown and gold interior, has previews of London productions, and one of the busiest hotels, the Majestic, built high on the hill in 1900, with its huge windows and imposing pillars in the interior, has murals in the lounge depicting eighteenth-century scenes in various spa towns.

If you feel like a short drive, only a few miles from Harrogate is the decorative village of Ripley. Inspired by Alsace-Lorraine, the cobbled streets, the arched Gothic windows of the cottages built in 1827, the Hotel de Ville, the bridle road and the plunging waterfall make an almost theatrical background to Ripley Castle. The gatehouse of 1418 leads to this fortified stronghold, originally designed to withstand the frequent raids of the Scottish General Black Douglas. Today the library, where Lady Ingleby received Cromwell after the battle of Marston Moor with two pistols stuck into her belt, the Knights' Chamber, with a priest's hole in the sixteenth-century panelling, the Cromwellian boots casually left behind after the battle, the family tombs defaced in the church by Cromwell's troops, and the massive treasure-chest, with its thirty-two-fold lock worked by one enormous key, remind one forcibly of the terrors and uncertainties of the Civil War.

The ceiling of the Tower Room with its plasterwork of fleur-de-lys, the Lion of Scotland and the boar's head crest of the Ingilbys, put up in 1603 for the visit of James I; the jerkins of cowhide, which could deflect a broadsword, issued to Sir William Ingleby's private troop of horse; the finely-chased sixteenth-century royal armour made at Greenwich, comparable in quality to that in the Wallace Collection; the portrait of Francis Ingleby, who was hung, drawn and quartered by order of Queen Elizabeth I for his activities as a Jesuit Priest; the graceful Canova sculpture of Aphrodite in the Drawing-Room, and the picture on panel of Edward III, whose life was saved during a boar hunt in 1355 by Thomas Ingleby, combine to show us an historical vista through the activities of this remarkable family, whose ancestor Robert de Engelbi came to England with the army of William the Conqueror, and whose descendants have lived for 600 years in the same house.

To the east of Ripley is the market town of Knaresborough, where horse-drawn carriages took visitors from Harrogate down Gracious Street to see the river Nidd,

Mother Shipton's cave and the Dropping Well, in which objects are turned to stone by the petrifying action of the water. Inhabitants of this ancient town, owned by Edward the Confessor before the Norman Conquest, fell victim to the Black Death in 1349, which for some years affected the efficiency of the local farming. Knaresborough Castle, of which today only a part of the ruined keep survives, was an important political and strategic factor in the policies of King John towards the Scots and the rebellious barons, and while the castle was strengthened at great expense, weapons such as crossbow bolts, called quarrels, were made in the town.

French faïence centrepiece in the Royal Baths café

By the end of the eighteenth century, when the manufacture of linen had become the main industry, two steam-powered mills were set up during the Napoleonic Wars, and in 1818 Thomas Telford was asked to investigate the possibility of a canal. The canal was never built, but it was the railways in 1848 which increased prosperity by bringing coal and flax to Knaresborough, besides tens of thousands of visitors each year to the expanding spa town of Harrogate. In recent times, coins of Roman Emperors have been found in the area, and today the tier upon tier of cottages built upon the rocks which overlook the Nidd as it passes through a deep gorge, where there are boats for hire near the waterside walk, Mother Shipton's beer garden with a view of the swans on the river, names like the Drip-Drop-Shoppe and a public house with the unusual name of The Borough Bailiff, make this a fascinating town.

I once stayed with friends in a house at Walshaw, near Halifax, on the moors which are the setting for Emily Brontë's *Wuthering Heights*, where the passionate, vindictive Heathcliff searched for his adored Catherine. It was a lonely place, windswept and rather frightening, and I remember we had a picnic lunch with a tart made of bilberries which grow wild in those parts. Afterwards we went to Haworth, to see the parsonage where the Rev. Patrick Brontë, originally Brunty from Co. Down, lived with his three daughters and one son, Branwell, and locked the front door at nine o'clock each night, when the girls' Celtic imaginations ran riot into words penned in tiny notebooks. Charlotte's hardstone brooch, the uncomfortable horsehair sofa in the dining-room, and the polished pine handrail on the stairs are a few of the sparse details which survive to sum up for us the restricted life of those talented sisters in that isolated place.

As you approach Haworth today on the Bradford road, there is a tall aqueduct near Cullingworth, and at the bottom of the hill water tumbles over the rocks. Houses seem to cling to the very edge of the valleys; there are dry stone walls and heather on the moors, and at last, after the steep incline of Black Moor road, you can see the gabled station of the Worth Valley Railway and the Bridgehouse Mills. The centre of the village lies at the top of cobbled Bridgehouse Lane, past the cosy Stirrup restaurant, the Craft Centre, and the Horseshoe Gallery. Then there is the parish church of St Michael of All Angels with its home-made prayer tree inside, and outside the parsonage which faces the forbidding churchyard, with ranks of flat graves, some slightly tilted, giving the impression that in a short while the painting by Stanley Spencer, *The Resurrection*, could come to life and souls emerge from beneath their stone prisons.

From Haworth we went into Keighley, where there are still unadopted roads where grass grows between rows of houses, past the mills, then through wooded valleys towards the sheep town of Skipton, capital of the district of Craven. The open market in the High Street, the cobbles in Cook's Yard, the pedimented Town Hall of 1862, the low-scale houses, and the well-kept eighteenth-century offices of Charlesworth and Foster, Solicitors, are a suitably restrained backdrop for the drama of Skipton Castle.

The fourteenth-century Gatehouse has a handsome balustrade, added in the seventeenth century, which proclaims '*Désormais*' the motto of the Clifford family. The watch-tower, like a huge drum, has arrow loops cut in the upper room, and the romantic Conduit Court, a sheltered inner courtyard with a yew tree in the centre, a place for troubadours to serenade their ladies, leads up to the Banqueting Hall, conveniently adjacent to the old kitchens, with deep bread ovens used for over 300 years.

I had always wanted to see Bolton Priory, founded in 1151, of which Ruskin wrote in glowing terms, and at a bend in the road which runs down from Grassington and Burnsall we were not disappointed by the sudden, dazzling view of the arched ruins enclosing the parish church. On the left runs the river Wharfe in which are embedded fifty-seven stepping stones to act as a ford for those who wish to reach the dale which rises from the opposite bank. Brown and white flecked Jacob sheep, with curled horns, graze in front of the Priory, and a miniature aqueduct which spans the road used to carry water to the corn mills.

The twisting road to Pateley Bridge reveals a wild and rocky landscape, but when we began the descent from the top of Greenhow Hill, the sun came out, emphasising the pale grey of the dry stone walls, and lighting up a vast panorama of green hills and the dark crags of Nidderdale. At the bottom of the valley the park has a pavilion near the sheltered tennis courts, and the bright shops in the upper part of the town include a hand-engraver of crystal in Old Church Lane and an antique shop, The Cat in the Window, where not only were the gleaming eyes of a pottery cat seen through the glass, but customers are confronted by the baleful glare of a fox's mask. We had a picnic beside the river in this charming market town, which was given its charter by Edward II and called after a 'pate', the local term for a badger.

Near Ripon is one of the finest monastic ruins in Europe, Fountains Abbey. In 1132 thirteen Benedictine monks moved from York to land granted by Archbishop Thurstan in remote, thorny Skelldale, and despite spending the first winter sheltering under an elm tree before graduating to wooden huts, they started to build an abbey which slowly grew during the twelfth century, so that eventually sheep farming and lead-mining were part of the extensive estates of this strict Cistercian order. Today the high Perpendicular Tower, the Refectory, the Warming-Room, the entrance arches of the Chapter House, and the Cellarium, with its stone vaults, all present an authentic picture of an important religious house. The setting, near Fountains Hall, which was built in the eighteenth century with stones from the lay-brothers' infirmary at the Abbey, is in a valley beside the river Skell which provided water for brewing, washing and drainage, and surrounded by mature woods and smooth lawns. At dusk it is deserted, haunting, mysterious, and, when seen through a mist, a suitable subject for the nineteenth-century painter Atkinson Grimshaw; yet it evokes, by its survival, the faith and tenacity of those monks of long ago.

In contrast, if you enter the cathedral at Ripon, built of millstone grit, through

Ackrill's Printers in Montpelier Parade, which once published a weekly list of visitors to the Spa

the door in the impressive west front, you immediately feel that it is a warm, welcoming place. I was not surprised to learn that it is all at once a cathedral, a minster, and used as a parish church, where marriages are performed with regularity. Despite the disproportionate width of the nave there is a feeling of intimacy created by the pinnacled canopies of the choir-stalls, begun in 1489; by the delicately carved reredos with figures of saints outlined against the east window, one of the finest examples of geometrical tracery in England; by the colourful screen; the curious misericords; the gilded thirteenth-century bosses on the later wooden vaulting of the choir roof; the Nollekens sculpture in the south transept; and the medieval font, often used for christenings. The Norman chapter house contains the vestments and the illuminated charter of James I which restored the church revenues sequestrated in 1545. It is an adventure to descend to the Saxon crypt built in 672 and squeeze along a narrow aperture which opens out at intervals to reveal lighted alcoves where plate is displayed from the Cathedral and nearby parish churches. There is an alms dish encrusted with garnets, an Anglo-Saxon brooch, discovered in 1978, a silver flagon of 1675, a jewelled chalice, and countless pieces of church silver replacing the relics of saints wrapped in gold leaf which were carefully guarded here in former times. The enterprising wife of the Dean welcomes visitors to this living church, which during special concerts resounds to music of the Italian Renaissance, to Monteverdi's Vespers, and to the orchestras of the Northern Philharmonic or the English Sinfonia.

Only a few miles beyond the outskirts of the town are some of the finest interiors in Europe, at Newby Hall. In 1767 Robert Adam was commissioned by William Weddell to redecorate the earlier house as a suitable background for the sculpture, furniture and other treasures which he had bought on his travels abroad. The

Sample bottles of Spa water

Opposite Exercise pool in the Turkish Baths

Gobelins tapestries in narrow gilt frames of *Les Amours de Dieu*, from cartoons by Boucher, are complemented by the graceful plaster arabesques of the Tapestry Room ceiling, with medallions painted by Zucchi, by the carpet in subtle shades of pink, grey and gold, and by the classical motifs carved on the dark mahogany doors.

Many of Adam's recurring features in houses such as Osterley or Mellerstain were derived from the Emperor Diocletian's Palace at Split, which he visited when a young man, and here the magnificence of the plasterwork in the Library executed by Joseph Rose, the Entrance Hall with its appliqués of martial trophies, the Sculpture Gallery where the Barberini Venus stands in a niche of which the coved upper part is decorated with the lightness of sugar icing, confirm Adam as one of the greatest designers of all time.

Many historic houses are seen, alas, because of the straitened circumstances of their owners, with torn wallpaper, furniture badly in need of cleaning and restoration, and tatty curtains and lampshades, an appearance far removed from the original concept. How refreshing, therefore, to be shown at Newby the Drawing Room, with its ceiling newly painted in the original colours of avocado, pink and dark red based on the drawing in the Soane Museum, to see the frieze restored to dark red and white, and below it the striped wallpaper against which the Lawrence portrait is perfectly attuned, and to admire the symmetrical arrangement of the inlaid satinwood furniture, upon which lamps, small boxes, photographs and china have been placed by the owners with a careful eye for detail.

The elaborate four-poster beds draped with chintz in glowing colours, the pretty Motto Bedroom with sayings painted on the walls and furniture, the more sober Homer Room with hunting scenes by Sartorius, have all been restored with loving care, in unerring and highly individual style. Those rooms also demonstrate the hopeless task faced by committees, however well meaning, who increasingly act as patrons of the arts, or curators of houses or museums, when anything involving taste or imagination comes up for discussion.

Yorkshire has many facets. *Eboracum* was the Roman capital of the north, and from this county have emerged world-famous men. Captain Cook, the boy from Whitby who, on his voyage in the *Endeavour*, opened up Australia and the Pacific Ocean: giants of industry like Lord Mackintosh of Halifax; cricketers such as Len Hutton or Geoffrey Boycott, and Harold Wilson, who was born in Huddersfield.

From Harrogate the traveller is offered endless permutations. If I have neglected Harewood, where Chippendale carved pelmets to look like silken draperies, and where the clair-de-lune Chinese porcelain mounted in ormolu is a joy to behold; or Nostell, a great mansion by James Paine and Adam, near Wakefield; or York, where the shock of pleasure one feels at that first sight of the circular Rose window in the Minster, and the fun of walking down Stonegate and Petergate, are unforgettable experiences, it is purely for lack of space to record all the cultural riches of this vast area, which I hope you will discover for yourselves.

MALVERN SPA

When Elgar returned to Malvern in 1891, his walks over the hills, where he often flew his kite, inspired him to write the *Enigma Variations*. His father had been the proprietor of a Pianoforte and Music Warehouse at 10, High Street, Worcester, and he also tuned pianos in houses such as Croome Court or Madresfield. Young Edward would go with him, and wander round the gardens or talk to the grooms while he waited. In later years, before graduating to a two-seater car, he explored the villages of Worcestershire on his bicycle, and there is a photograph which shows him propped against his machine, with a bowler hat, leather gloves, a high-buttoned jacket and a serious expression, not unlike the riders of today in their pin-striped suits who are determined to defeat the London rush-hour traffic to the City.

Elgar was born at Broadheath, within sight of the Malvern Hills, and while a struggling composer he gave music lessons, and subsequently married one of his pupils, Alice Roberts, the daughter of a Major-General who lived in the Worcestershire village of Redmarley. *The Dream of Gerontius* was written at Craig Lea, the Elgars' house at Malvern, and in 1929 the first of the yearly Malvern Festivals cemented the friendship between Elgar and George Bernard Shaw. To this day, the creative genius of both the musician and the playwright seem to permeate the cultural life of the town.

If you approach Malvern from Worcester through Madresfield and Malvern Link, there is a feeling of relaxation, that you need not hurry past the stone walls behind which the handsome detached houses seem remote and unchanged from a hundred years ago. The commons are planted with trees, there are seats conveniently placed to achieve the best views of the hills, and the road winds steadily upwards through Barnards Green to Church Street, then curls round to Belle Vue Terrace and along to Malvern Wells.

In the centre of the town are the Winter Gardens, where the famous spa water pours into immense cans of polished brass from a fountain of four bronze babies, and where on the terrace visitors from many countries stroll during the interval of plays, concerts or operas which are performed in the adjacent theatre. The sloping gardens, with seats of green wrought iron, a mulberry tree planted by Shaw, and a newly reinstated bandstand restored by individuals each paying two pounds towards a brick, lead down to the lake which was once a fishpond for the monks

The Winter Gardens

Runnings Park Hotel

who lived at the Priory. An elaborate bridge of slatted oak, with heavy wooden newels, reaches across the water in which there are weeping willows and white Aylesbury ducks. The Grange, Victorian Gothic, painted creamy beige and white, Priory Park Mansion and other private houses can be seen from this peaceful garden between the cedars, the wellingtonias and the dove and maidenhair trees from China.

Priory Park Mansion, built by a doctor in 1874 and now used by the Council Treasurer, has an ecclesiastical front door with granite pillars, and the main staircase, with newels carved to represent heraldic beasts, leads to a brightly-coloured stained-glass window on which there are emerald-green frogs, herons with pink legs eating small fishes, blue dragon-flies, yellow sunflowers and a fox with one eye closed, perhaps winking at this fantasia of colour and design. In the passage more stained glass shows mice eating corn and hydrangeas with green leaves burgeoning from flower pots, while on the inlaid floor St Wulstan is depicted receiving the Charter for Malvern.

The Priory Church, once inhabited by Benedictine monks, was bought for £20 by

Opposite Bust of Elgar silhouetted against the Priory Church

Tudor monument of Anne Knotsford in the Priory Church

---

the people of Malvern from Henry VIII during the Dissolution of the Monasteries. This impressive building has fine Tudor monuments of John and Jane Knotsford carved from alabaster in 1589. Their daughter Anne, with chiselled features like a portrait of Queen Elizabeth I, in an embroidered dress with elaborate cuffs, a ruff, and bedecked with necklaces, kneels in front of a prie-dieu which has a tasselled cushion laid on a fringed cloth. The fifteenth-century wall tiles of fishes, dragons and pelicans in pink, gold and lavender form the largest surviving collection in the country, and the early stained glass of the same period, with a group of angel musicians in the East window, is in soft shades of yellow and brown.

From the churchyard entrance, where stone pillars support an iron lantern, a lane leads us past the wine merchants at Littleton House to Cridlam and Walker, who are the unusual combination of fruiterers and butchers, in an ornamental Regency Gothic building which has the original green and white tiles, railings topped by pointed spears, and a wheelbarrow brimming over with flowers in the paved courtyard in front of the attached house. Next to the shop is the Priory Gatehouse, with an oval window and battlements, once used by the monks and later as staff quarters for the old inn on the site of the Abbey Hotel, where coaches stopped on their way to London.

At the top of Church Street the newly cleaned building of Barclays Bank leads the eye up to the height of Belle Vue Terrace. The Regency frontage of the Foley Arms Hotel; the Victorian Gothic building at number forty-six with its maroon front door; the baskets of flowers outside Adelaide House; the inviting doorways of Warwick House, one of the most renowned local shops; and views towards Gloucestershire and Herefordshire between unusual buildings which are now small guest houses or hotels, make one echo the words of John Evelyn in 1654 when he praised Malvern for having 'one of the goodliest vistas in England'.

It was Dr Wall, perhaps more famous as the founder of the Worcester Porcelain Works, who in the 1750s promoted the waters of St Ann's Well and the Holy Well, both of which were known to early missionaries, who used them to baptise their converts to the Christian faith. Dr Wall began to attract fashionable patients after the publication of his treatise on the merits of Malvern water, and sure-footed donkeys carried sufferers up the steep roads to the Wells. Princess Victoria rode on a donkey named Royal Moses, and Charles Dickens, a visitor in 1851, poked fun at the keen young men 'dashing down the hills', presumably the equivalent of those relentless joggers of our own time.

Dr Wilson and Dr Gully, who arrived at Malvern in 1842, devised an onerous routine of 'Lamp Baths', 'Sitz Baths', and the dreaded 'Douche', whereby fifty gallons of ice-cold water was discharged over the wretched patient, causing some to scream and others to collapse on the ground. The régime had to be strictly followed, and the novelist Lord Lytton, tempted into buying six rich tarts at a pastry-cook's, was caught by Dr Wilson and made to throw his purchases uneaten into the gutter.

Balls, excursions, public breakfasts, beds in hotels for one shilling and sixpence a day, advertisements for a new Restorative Hair Fluid, painless improvements for Artificial Teeth, and an ever-present chorus of beggars, charlatans and tricksters were the side-effects of fashionable spa life in Malvern. By the 1870s the tumult and the shouting died, and the doctors had departed, their gullible patients gone abroad to seek cures of a less spartan nature, accompanied by the delights of gambling.

In 1862 a new impetus was given to the fortunes of the town by the founding of Malvern College, built by the brother of Joseph Hansom, who invented the cab of that name. As one stands today in College Road and looks down at the variety of buildings, including the distinguished Memorial Library of Sir Aston Webb, the general impression is of a rambling palace whose turrets, spires, battlements, arches and gables seem more appropriate to an eastern potentate than for the use of young boys. But the masters' houses, some with gardens and even orchards, continue the feeling that the buildings of Malvern are merely temporarily superimposed on the side of the hills, which, being formed of a stratum over 400 million years ago, have a permanence denied to the work of any architect, however distinguished or successful.

My favourite building in Malvern is the station. Built in 1861, the clock with Roman numerals, the stained glass in the waiting-room, and the benches with the

The Holy Well and (*opposite*) the house built over it

proud initials G.W.R. bear witness to an age when it was not only an adventure, but often a pleasure, to travel by train. On the platform, the wrought-iron supports of the glass canopy are surmounted by coronets out of which rise bunches of acorns, chestnuts, and large stylised leaves, all of which have been repainted in their original colours of lime green, red, orange and yellow, while the pillars are in pale grey. The bold cast-iron tracery of this period is painted white, and throws into focus the red of the doors, a combination which makes the station a bright and happy place from which to start a holiday.

I can remember so many arrivals, fraught with delicious anticipation, to find my diminutive grandmother waiting for me. She often wore a jacket and skirt in burgundy red, with a hat to match pulled well down over her grey curls, grey lisle stockings covering her slim ankles, furs of stone marten round her shoulders, and a garnet bar brooch securing the red chiffon scarf wound about her neck. She always had exciting plans arranged for our time together. There would be a party, with organised games and competitions, at which even the most inept would win armfuls of prizes, so that nobody would be disappointed. There would be a bring-and-buy in the village, blackberrying on the common, tennis with friends at Colwall, and once we went to the pantomime in Birmingham, where Douglas Byng, resplendent as the Dame, sang 'The Stately Homes of England'.

Granny lived at Poolbrook, just outside Malvern, in a timbered house, painted

black and white, with a rose garden, a swimming pool, installed for my uncles, and an orchard, which in this fertile Vale of Evesham seemed to provide an endless supply of apples, plums, pears and even cider fruit, all of which were carefully picked, graded, eaten, or sold, and provided a helpful addition to Granny's income.

One of my uncles was a happy-go-lucky regular soldier, the other a serious politician. Their books, all available to me, were therefore a mixture of G. A. Henty, Edgar Wallace, Conrad and Robert Louis Stevenson, or the lives and speeches of Gladstone and Disraeli. My happiest hours were spent mentally following the Moloch of Midlothian through his campaigns, or embroiled in a desperate battle in China with G. A. Henty, while I sat hidden away in an arbour in the rose garden at the foot of the Malvern Hills.

Sometimes we went to have luncheon or tea with the Beauchamps at Madresfield Court. This moated house of Elizabethan brick with stepped gables, an interior courtyard, a minstrels' gallery, and filled with unusual treasures, always seemed to me the epitome of glamour and romance. On one occasion, when I was older, Walter Monckton and his wife were staying there, and I was fascinated to meet this world-famous lawyer, later Minister of Labour, with the sharp brain and gentle, sympathetic voice.

When I was fifteen I went to a birthday party at Ledbury, where today Church Lane, with timbered houses overhanging the cobbled street, is a magnet for visitors. Then it was a sleepy place, and my friends the Biddulphs lived in a square Georgian house, where for the party competitions had been painstakingly devised beforehand, such as having to guess how many beans in a bottle, or being asked to fill in the brand name of a product which had been carefully cut out of a newspaper advertisement. We thoroughly enjoyed these simple pleasures, and I was delighted with my new long dress, with puff sleeves, made of flowered ersatz silk bought in a roll off a stall in Bedford Market.

Once or twice Granny took me to Pershore, where she had lived at Amerie Court, and when I returned recently, it seemed unchanged and beautifully cared for in every detail. It was a joy to notice the lack of plastic shop fascias or garish neon lighting, as in some other country towns.

The Royal Three Tuns Hotel, with painted barrels outside, is in a dominant position in the High Street, where the low-scale Georgian houses blend well together to create a sense of harmony. Above the ironmonger and chemist are canopies with wrought-iron balconies. Numbers seventy and seventy-two have curved window-guards on the first floor, and Stanhope House has steps on either side to reach the raised front door, painted black, with a highly-polished brass handle and door knocker. Barclays Bank has an elaborate pierced fanlight, Fern House has a door of bright emerald green, and through the archway which leads to the Millside Boatyard there are glimpses of the River Avon. The grandest building is Perrott House, now an antique shop, built in 1760 by Judge Perrott, a Baron of the Exchequer, the interior of which is decorated with elaborate stucco work.

In Bridge Street, the Baptist Chapel of 1888, with its carved mottoes of Faith, Hope, Peace and Charity, leads the eye towards the double-fronted house at the end with arched Venetian windows, and on around the corner to Pershore Abbey. Founded by King Oswald in 689, it was built in 1090, and has a fourteenth-century lantern tower with slender spires emerging from corner turrets. Inside, you immediately feel the friendly atmosphere. The simple Norman font, taken away and used for many years as a cattle trough, the careful craftsmanship of the vaulted roof, the three great arches which frame the altar and the painted Haslewood monument of 1624 are admired by the flow of visitors and residents who come to this Abbey. The cottages, shops and small hotels which encircle the surrounding gardens ensure that the Abbey is part of the life of the town and not, as with less accessible churches, entered out of duty at infrequent intervals, or kept locked against strangers.

Not far to the west of Pershore is Upton-on-Severn, where boats can be hired on the river near the timber-framed Old Anchor Inn of 1601, which adjoins the black and white painted Butcher's Shop at number seven High Street. This town has great charm, and there are many historic buildings which are now shops selling books, antiques, prints or curios, some half-timbered, some with leaves and flowers of stucco below the parapet like the Old Court House of 1668 in New Street, which soon peters out into fields from which there are superb views of the Malvern Hills. The delicatessen on the corner of Court Street, the Malthouse in Waterside and the vet's house in Minge Lane are all a pleasure to look at, but the most striking feature of the town is the curious Bell Tower. This is all that remains of the early church of 1300, but in 1769 the architect Anthony Keck built an addition to the top in the shape of an octagon, painted green and white, with small round windows, and surmounted by a cupola made of copper, a cousin of the grander versions in Bavaria at Wies or Ettal.

Near Upton is Hanley Castle, where the Three Kings public house stands behind a grassy area with a seat placed beneath an old cedar tree, and where timber-framed almshouses of 1600 overlook the churchyard and the church with its simple Norman doorway.

It is so agreeable to make a relaxed tour of these small Worcestershire towns and villages with their unhurried atmosphere and timbered buildings which are a foil to the trees and orchards, especially when the blossom is in bloom.

As a complete contrast, to the north of Malvern are the ruins of Great Witley. From a long way away, one can see high on the hill the shell of a huge pillared house, of which the balustrade, topped by stone vases of flowers, is silhouetted against the sky. Inside the courtyard are arched Venetian windows, and the wings which thrust out over the brow of the hill must once have held rooms with views spreading over several counties. There are the remains of Jacobean towers from a house belonging to the Russell family, altered in 1683 by Thomas Foley, and in 1860 Samuel Dawkes was commissioned to enlarge and embellish the existing fabric by the first Earl of Dudley. During his minority, the house was used by Queen Adelaide, widow of the Sailor King, William IV. The two-storey entrance portico with Ionic columns, the Orangery like an Italian villa, the garden with its prancing horse in the Perseus Fountain, and the Triton Fountain, where strange sea-people blow silent music from their shells, combine to create a setting of great magnificence.

There is an old photograph of the Ballroom, encrusted with gilded plasterwork, and hung on either side with rows of massive chandeliers reflected in mirrored alcoves, where the settees and chairs covered in cut velvet, and a piano in the centre, appear to wait for the huge double doors at the end of the room to be flung open to allow the ladies in crinolines and their bewhiskered escorts in white ties, tailcoats and wearing carnations to assemble after dinner for a short concert given by Jenny Lind or Tetrazzini. It is all over, yet these ruins have their own unassailable dignity, echoes of Ozymandias – 'Look on my works, ye mighty, and despair.'

The white and gold Italianate church, with graceful ceiling paintings of 1654 by Antonio Bellucci, and a dramatic monument to Lord Foley by Rysbrack, is a further surprise in the sparsely inhabited countryside. The glow of the stained glass fashioned by Joshua Price in 1719, the glitter of the madonna lilies set in a gold mosaic background behind the altar, the deeply carved ends of the pews, the white marble font and the baroque pulpit are an unusual combination to find in England; yet it has a warmth and lightness conducive both to prayer and gratitude for blessings bestowed.

Returning towards Malvern you can visit the cathedral city of Worcester, sacked by Romans, Danes and Saxons, whose city walls were destroyed by Cromwell's troops in 1651. Inside the Cathedral the impressive early Norman Crypt was built in 1084 by St Wulfstan, and from the plain capitals rise sturdy semi-circular arches to support the ceiling. The cricket ground and the racecourse are on the meadows below the bridge, and the Guildhall of 1721, designed by a pupil of Wren, has statues of Charles I and his eldest son flanking the entrance, while the head of Cromwell is shown nailed by the ears. Visitors come from far and near to see the craftsmen at work in Dr Wall's Worcester Porcelain Works, from which fine bone china is still exported to many different countries.

In Malvern I was interested to see flowers and birds being sculpted and painted by hand for the delicate china sprays and groups achieved by Boehm. It is firms such as this, as well as the Morgan Car Company and the Technical Research Establishment, where technicians experiment to perfect new radar techniques, which have boosted the economy of Malvern, and encouraged business and commerce.

Each year thousands of visitors arrive to see for themselves the Severn Valley or the spires of Hereford Cathedral from the top of the Malvern Hills. The painted curlicues on the gabled houses, the old gas lamps in Wells Road and the pillar boxes of the epoch of Edward VII, are all details which linger in the mind. As one takes the steep road towards Malvern Wells or Malvern Link, or to St Ann's Well, where long ago the baptisms took place, and nearer our own time pupils from Malvern Girls' College used to climb up to the café nearby, which was out of bounds, one can be glad that these hills have continued to attract and inspire great men and women, and that many of their achievements are known throughout the world.

ROYAL LEAMINGTON SPA

I N THIS WARWICKSHIRE TOWN , Greek Doric porches and fluted Ionic columns greet the eye and soothe the senses. Modern shops have been carefully integrated into the irreplaceable Regency façades; and residents are proud of their rose-filled gardens in front of white stuccoed villas, built in the 1830s, against which black-painted wrought iron in patterns of acanthus leaves, shells, or interlocking diamonds and ovals seems like a trimming of black lace.

Just beside Victoria Bridge which spans the River Leam, and through the Italianate entrance lodges, are Jephson Gardens, where you can wander towards the temple and the sparkling fountains in the centre of the lake, between beds of dahlias, scented plants and rare shrubs. The aviary holds love-birds, finches and parakeets; Russian hickory, alder and tulip-trees are planted among many unusual species in these thirteen acres right in the centre of the town. There are swans, shelduck and Canada geese, and below the blue and white suspension bridge boys fish in the weir, where yearly raft races take place in the summer.

The gardens were once a strip of meadow, which in 1834 was first used for an Archery Tournament. Two years later, the owner, Mr Willes, gave the land on a 2,000-year lease at a peppercorn rent, to become 'a public pleasure ground'. The lake was laid out, arbours and summer-houses erected, and in 1848 a row of memorial oaks was planted, together with many of the trees and shrubs which have now grown to maturity. A temple and a fountain followed, and the gardens were named after the popular Doctor Jephson, a benefactor of the town.

Just outside, the Pump Room, with its Tuscan colonnade, was opened in 1814. Today coffee, light luncheons and free spa water are offered to visitors, while at the rear over 60,000 treatments including hydrotherapy take place each year.

There were references to the springs of Leamington as early as 1586, and a hundred years later Dr Guidott of Bath declared the water to be 'nitrous', contradicted in 1740 by Dr Short, who described it as a 'mere brine spring', until in 1757 Dr Rutty compromised by calling it a 'salino-nitreous spring'. But whatever the taste or content, the first spring flowed from a fissure in the rock beside the Parish Church, and various attempts to build a bath-house were abortive. In 1782, William Abbotts, landlord of the Black Dog Inn, with his crony Benjamin Satchwell, discovered by chance a second spring on his own land, and after having the water analysed by Dr Kerr, the leading physician in Northampton, who praised it, Abbotts started to build baths and a new lodging house.

The Royal Pump Room and Baths

In a few years visitors could use baths belonging to Mr Abbotts, Mr Wise or Mrs Curtis. Later there were the marble baths of Mr Robbins, and those of the Rev. Mr Read, but in 1812 a local syndicate commissioned Smith of Warwick to build the impressive new Pump Room and Baths which we can see today, which over-shadowed the others, and to which was added the royal prefix.

The Corporation restricted the height to thirty feet, conscious even in those times of the importance of achieving the right scale in relation to the surrounding area. Doric pillars, the Pump with a basin of Derbyshire marble enclosed by a mahogany balustrade, and chimneypieces with marble from Kilkenny, were some of the grand architectural features. An orchestra played while visitors drank the waters, and in the adjacent gardens an avenue of linden trees was planted to give shade to the crowds who came to listen to the military band and to stroll beside the river Leam. Nowadays you can still admire the blue and white bandstand topped by a gilded finial, archways of wrought iron with crowns, maple trees, cedars, and beds of bright flowers, which lead the eye to the river, where disabled people can fish from a specially-constructed platform.

In the year the Pump Room opened, the population of Leamington numbered only 1,800, and more hotels were urgently needed to cope with the new arrivals anxious to try the saline waters.

The Bedford had opened in 1811, where the Corinthian, Jack Mytton, was challenged by a wager to ride his mare upstairs into the dining-room, jump over the table, and on over the balcony to the street below. He won the bet. From the mews at the rear, the London coach *Nimrod*, and the *Imperial*, destined for Cheltenham, would set off daily. One unusual event held at the hotel in 1812, was a raffle, for those who were prepared to buy five-guinea tickets, of a three-bedroomed freehold house in Union Street.

The Stoneleigh Hotel opened in 1812. The Crown and the Blenheim followed, and in 1818 came Williams Hotel in Union Parade, a palatial building with an entrance facing the elm trees in front of Denby Villa, later replaced in 1883 by the massive red-brick Town Hall, with obelisks on the roof, windows decorated with stained glass and inlaid mosaics on the façade.

View across the River Leam

Mr and Mrs Williams had been butler and housekeeper to the Greatheeds, a local family, and they decided to use their knowledge of the requirements of landed gentlemen, like the first proprietors of London hotels such as Browns and Claridges, by catering for the needs of travellers who at the beginning of the nineteenth century were increasingly on the move. Acting upon the financial advice of the Greatheeds, they chose Smith of Warwick as the architect, and only a year later served turtle and venison at the banquet to celebrate the opening. Within three weeks the Prince Regent, staying at nearby Warwick for the Races, drove over to Leamington to see the town, and agreed that this splendid new hotel should be renamed the Regent, and bear his coat of arms.

In 1830, eleven-year-old Princess Victoria waved to the crowds from a window on the first floor, and when she became Queen, allowed the town to be renamed Royal Leamington Spa. Fashionable visitors such as the Duke and Duchess of Bedford visited the first playhouse, known as 'The Temple of Drama', where Macready was one of the leading performers besides Jenny Lind, the 'Swedish Nightingale'. Sarah Siddons and the Keans were other well-known theatrical

Jephson Gardens

Houses in Newbold Terrace

figures who visited Leamington, and for another thirty years the spa prospered, until the fashion for continental travel and the onset of the Crimean War. Today, Leamington retains the style and composure of a beautiful older woman who has known love and admiration and still expects it.

In Newbold Terrace the houses have shutters on the outside of the windows in the French manner, and steps lead up to the raised front doors, while on the first floor a canopy with arched supports of delicate wrought iron hangs over the verandah. One of my favourite places is Clarendon Square, built in 1825, on whose west side Greek Doric porches adorn the classical façade. Perched on the pillars which flank the entrance to the short driveway, heraldic winged dragons with speared tails put out their forked tongues.

The Temple in Jephson Gardens

In Leam Terrace, a wide street lined with trees, there are villas set back in their own gardens, some of them Regency Gothic with pointed windows, and castellated details, while in Lansdowne Crescent the curved frontage was designed in the 1820s by W. Thomas. Tucked away at the rear are the enchanting Regency villas of Lansdowne Circus, built in pairs, which circle a central garden.

In the main street of many historic towns brash shop fascias have destroyed the old lettering and strike a jarring note, building lines encroach on to the pavement, balconies have disappeared, architraves have been lopped off, and other classical features, considered a nuisance or too expensive to repair, have unaccountably vanished over a period of time.

Fountains in Jephson Gardens

In Leamington, a continuous balcony of wrought iron runs along the upper part
of Victoria Terrace, built in 1836, above the florist, the chemist, the patisserie, as
well as the other shops which have a mutual building line, and this agreeable street
reflects the care and thought given by the Council and the residents over the years
to protect the architectural details of the buildings.

In the Parade, even stores with household names, which are sometimes able to
dictate their own terms to the Local Authority, have restrained fascias, and some of
the frontages are replicas of the original, thus retaining the symmetry of the design.
Everywhere you look there are whirls of wrought iron fashioned into canopies or

Above Advertisements

Opposite Boats in a backwater

window-guards, and along the length of the well-kept Clarendon Hotel, painted a gleaming white, runs a black-painted balcony formed of bold circular flowers, ringed by interlaced scrolls.

Fêtes, carnivals and concerts in the Pump Room gardens attract people of all ages. There is tennis, cricket and bowls in the eighteen-acre Victoria Park; plays, variety shows and wrestling in the Royal Spa Centre. In the Art Gallery there is fine Delft, antique glass and fragile silver lustre. You can admire the great avenue of trees in Beverley Road, and watch the chestnuts in Northumberland Road turning gold in the autumn, while at any time of year you can gaze at the classical architecture of the crescents, terraces and squares, or stroll through the peaceful oasis of Jephson gardens, where the trees, the fountains, the temple, the obelisk and the floral clock are all reminders of the generosity of those who strove unceasingly to promote the prosperity and success of this elegant Regency town.

Only a few miles away is Warwick, where in Smith Street, the timbered medieval houses, painted black and white, jostle for a place with seventeenth- and

eighteenth-century buildings. The tiny shops sell crafts, guns or second-hand books. Number eighteen, painted pale green and white, is a family butcher, and pots of violets and crates of oranges are stacked on the pavement from the fruit and flower shop beside the Roebuck public house. The mellow red brick of Landor House, the King's High School for Girls, built in 1692, is highlighted with stone facings, and has a carefully-polished sign and a brass letterbox.

In the High Street the larger Georgian houses have a pediment over the doors, and the Porridge Pot restaurant, built in 1420, where a cauldron hangs outside, has shining copper pots in the window. The impressive Court House, by Francis Smith, built in 1725 of rusticated stone, with Doric pilasters on the upper floor, has a niche over the door where Justice, holding her scales, guards the rights of those who enter. The pillared Midland Bank, the wrought-iron balcony over Silvester Antiques, which offers glass, china and silver, combine to make this an unusually attractive street, which leads to Westgate and the ancient Lord Leycester Hospital.

Its buildings, started in 1123, were originally used as a meeting place by the United Guilds of Warwick, combining the Guilds of St George the Martyr, the Holy Trinity and Mary the Virgin. The Members, from all trades, also acted as the first highway authority, in order to ensure that the roads were passable and commerce was attracted to the town.

In 1571, Robert, Earl of Leicester, favourite of Queen Elizabeth, decided to found a hospital for aged retainers and their wives, and even today eight ex-servicemen, known as Brethren, occupy the flats which have been converted from the old buildings. In the courtyard, where a brightly painted porcupine, a muzzled bear and other heraldic emblems feature on the black and white façade under the roof of red and grey tiles, early wooden arches support the galleried upper storey above the cloisters. An outside staircase leads to the Guildhall, where the small closet with a window, built into the high timbered roof, afforded a private meeting place for the Master and the bailiffs. There is a collection of swords from military campaigns, a wide brass collar which belonged to Lord Leicester's mastiff, and heavy copper beer cans, used for beer brewed in the adjacent Malthouse.

From the high stone balcony of the Chapel, built over Westgate, the entrance to Warwick from Stratford-upon-Avon, there are views right along the street towards the fifteenth-century Eastgate and the Chapel of St Peter.

As you pass through the Gatehouse of Warwick Castle, with its menacing portcullis, and see the battlemented walls and the twelve-sided Guy's Tower of 1394, you are not surprised to learn that the earlier castle was sacked by Simon de Montfort, and that both Guy's and Caesar's Towers were constructed to waylay advancing troops, who on the other side could only gain access by crossing the river and storming the battlements. A drawbridge, secret stairways, gun-ports in the Clarence and Bear Towers and the dungeons for captured prisoners made this fortified castle impregnable against even the most violent enemies or treacherous friends.

Inside, the state rooms recall the heyday of the Beauchamps and the Grevilles.

The Great Hall, with its checked floor of cream and burnt orange marble from Verona, has Italian jousting armour of 1540 and rare horse armour from Germany. The Cedar Drawing-Room, with panelled walls of Lebanese cedar-wood and a brown and gold Aubusson carpet, the carving by Grinling Gibbons in the Blue Boudoir, and the sixteenth-century table of pietra dura, inlaid with agate, jasper and lapis lazuli, bought from the Grimani Palace in Florence, are only a few of the treasures to be seen.

As a complete contrast, the private apartments show a house-party of the 1890s, given for the Prince of Wales by the radical Daisy, Countess of Warwick. In one room the waxwork figure of Dame Nellie Melba, accompanied by her pianist Signor Paolo Tosti, sings *Abide with me* to the Duchess of Devonshire and Jennie Jerome, mother of Winston Churchill. In the upstairs bathroom, complete with a sponge and Pears soap, a waxwork maid in a long frilled apron runs the water for Consuelo, Duchess of Marlborough, who is waiting in her negligée in the adjacent crimson damask bedroom; while the Prince of Wales, already changed for dinner and wearing the Garter star, holds a private conversation with George Curzon, about to be appointed Viceroy of India, in the Kenilworth bedroom, in which the carved panelling was originally made for Kenilworth Castle.

Kenilworth is now a magnificent red sandstone ruin, a few miles from Warwick, which dominates the surrounding countryside. Once used by Henry III, it became the seat of the powerful Simon de Montfort, and was later the home of John of Gaunt. It was in the Great Hall that Edward II was forced to renounce the crown. It was the background for masques and water tableaux with which Robert, Earl of Leicester sought to amuse Queen Elizabeth I; the revels included morris-dancing, bear-baiting, acrobatics by tumblers from Italy and the consumption of 320 hogsheads of beer.

Nearby is the fourteenth-century moated manor house of Baddesley Clinton, where in the sheltered courtyard the diamond pattern of the Ferrers' coat of arms is laid out in yellow marigolds and red salvias contained by neat borders of box. The Great Hall has a stone fireplace with male supporters, below which there are carved gargoyles and lions' masks. The panels of armorial glass in the windows trace the family history back to the seventeenth century, and in the intimate Dining Room the gateleg table, the plain oak chairs, and the unusual ironstone plates marked with an anchor and set on lace-edged linen, allow us to forget for a moment that this house also has a warren of priest's holes, which over the years sheltered many in holy orders who were prepared to die for their religion.

A few miles away is Packwood House, with its rare seventeenth-century tapestry of Leda and the Swan, and the panelled bedroom with its canopied Jacobean bed, where the Parliamentary General Ireton slept before the battle of Edgehill. Prince Rupert, commander of the Royalist forces, lodged at the Manor House, Wormleighton, home of Henry, Lord Spencer, who died the following year fighting for the King. On the morning of the battle, Prince Rupert ordered the house to be burnt down to prevent its capture by the Roundheads. Edgehill, fought on

Boys fishing in the weir   *Opposite* The River Leam

Sunday 23 October 1642, was the first battle of the Civil War. The battlefield, near the village of Radway, was flat, fertile ground, where today you can see an occasional farmhouse, a belt of conifers which marks the line of the next field, and thick woods on the neighbouring heights, called the Edge Hill. This vantage point was seized by Prince Rupert before sunrise affording him a view of the countryside as far as Kineton.

His formidable cavalry charge, which began at the trot and ended at the gallop, even on the low-lying marshy ground, initially routed the numerically superior Parliamentarians, but two of their brigades retrieved the situation. After mistakes by both sides, military historians conclude that Edgehill ended in a draw. In the final count the energy and panache of Prince Rupert could not defeat the well-drilled troops of Cromwell.

Warwickshire, in the heart of England, has often been at the centre of momentous events, and when we look at the buildings and the landmarks which remain in modern times, it is sometimes possible to recapture faint echoes – ghostly reflections – of great deeds, shabby tricks, kindness, charity, laughter and splendour, which are all part of our history and our survival.

LLANDRINDOD WELLS SPA

At the Victorian Festival in September the ladies wore long skirts and cameo brooches. Gentlemen sported striped jackets and boaters, or serious frockcoats and gold watch chains. Straw bonnets were trimmed with flowers, mittens were rediscovered, parasols were twirled. Attics were ransacked for jet and old lace, children in caps and knickerbockers looked like Little Lord Fauntleroy or the Artful Dodger, and fairy lights, bunting and flags decorated the streets of this spa town in Mid-Wales.

At the Bakehouse, dark-haired girls with smiling eyes and mob caps offered Welsh cakes and Welsh bread; there was Welsh whisky at the Wine Cellar; and Mr Millward the jeweller, in a saffron cutaway coat with a matching tall hat, displayed in his window silver, jewellery, clocks and antique fans. There was Welsh lamb at the shop of Mr Knill the butcher, who was resplendent in a blue bow tie and red-and-white striped apron, and the outfitter, Mr Vaughan Jones, showed his hand-written ledgers of the 1920s.

There were veteran cars, puppet shows, a lakeside fête, a *thé dansant*, a bowls tournament, and a tour of local hostelries by songsters and thespians.

If you arrive from England, you find near the Welsh border the timbered black-and-white houses which evoke the life and times of Harri Tudur, the victor of Bosworth field, who ascended the English throne as Henry VII, but in Llandrindod the tall houses are built of Ruabon brick, a rich terracotta, sometimes with stone facings, or with an inlaid pattern of yellow brick, and the woodwork of the steeply-pitched gables is painted blue, emerald green and black. The roofs are of Welsh slate, and balconies, turrets and curlicues often adorn the villas or hotels built in the 1890s.

In Park Crescent, Mr Johnson the Druggist, established in 1878, has retained his early shopfront of clouded glass with gilt lettering, and in the window are giant bottles filled with blue and amber liquid flanked by decorated containers for rhubarb and arrowroot. Inside the shop, rows of mahogany drawers with moulded glass handles were designed to dispense camphor, alum, cetraceum or manna.

In Temple Street the Hotel Metropole, with its unusual balustrade of Art Nouveau wrought iron, is painted sage green and white, and in the summer months visitors sit at tables in the gardens opposite, wander down to the Welsh craft shop or go to see the Automobile Palace. This is a treasure house where hung up on view

Local people in Victorian dress

The butcher's shop

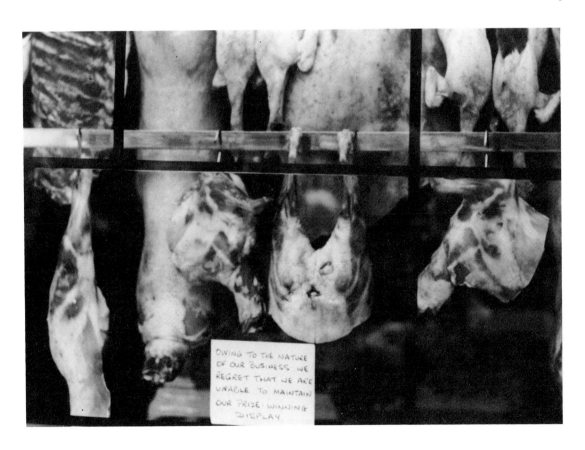

OWING TO THE NATURE
OF OUR BUSINESS, WE
REGRET THAT WE ARE
UNABLE TO MAINTAIN
OUR PRIZE-WINNING
DISPLAY.

The tailor

Happy Families

The butcher's boy

Bowling Greens in Rock Park

are Velocipedes, an Ariel of 1870, a Juno, a Penny Farthing and the remarkable Dursley Pederson. Tom Norton can tell you the history of each one, collected by his father, and explain the mysteries of differential gears, shaft drives and tangent spoked wheels.

In Rock Park, whose springs were recorded in the time of Charles II, the carefully restored Pump Room is constructed of black and cream bricks laid to resemble basket-work, and the exterior glass canopy is supported by slender columns of wrought iron, painted white, with decorative scrolls of dove grey. Here the medicinal waters are once again available, and there is a tea-room in the Edwardian style with comfortable basket chairs. A foot-bridge links the wooded paths above the stream, and the small black and cream lodges lead to the Bowling Greens with misty views of Powys and the Upper Wye Valley. There are walks down Lovers Leap on the River Ithon, or you can inhale the fresh, clear air while you stroll through the tree-lined streets of the town, where ivy-covered rocks jut out of the grassy slopes, and borders of shrubs grow above the low brick walls surrounding villas of red brick which often have stained glass set into their windows or front doors.

On 11 September 1935, Lloyd George wrestled with the Italo-Abyssinian situation in the old-fashioned telephone box of the Gwalia Hotel, now the Council Offices, using a torch and writing on a small ledge. That same evening he recalled to friends that it was his speech at Blaenau Ffestiniog in 1885 on the subject of Home Rule which had launched his parliamentary career. He was a frequent visitor to Llandrindod, as were the earlier travellers who arrived by coach in the Georgian period, and in Victorian times the building of the railway brought thousands of sufferers to drink the waters at a penny a glass.

Nowadays the active can test their strength on the demanding golf course, the highest in Wales, where the last hole requires a drive of 180 yards over the road, or walk on these heights above the town, which afford long views over Radnor Forest, towards the Roman Fort which tops Cefnllys Hill. On the twisting road below, the Queen of the Gypsies lies buried in a churchyard filled with white marble angels, and beyond, the fourteen-acre lake has rustic seats for those who want to watch the boating, or the fishing for carp and perch.

About seven miles away, an arched stone bridge leads into Builth Wells, where on the spacious showground the Royal Welsh Agricultural Society holds its annual show, attended by thousands of farmers, buyers, and those attracted by the different events.

At all times of the year people go to the Wyeside Centre, an unusual building of 1877, surmounted by a clock and a weather vane, which houses an art gallery, a restaurant and an indoor market held on Mondays, when stalls fill the vaulted cellars.

It was on a secret visit to Builth that Llywelyn ap Gruffydd, the last native Prince of Wales, sought refuge with a relative, the Governor of the Castle, in order to escape the pursuing forces of Edward I. Betrayed by his enemies, he fled to a nearby cave, but he was caught and beheaded. Today, a few miles from Builth at Cefn-y-Bedd, his simple memorial is a slab of rough-hewn Welsh stone which points to the sky.

Beyond Rhayader, with its stone clock-tower, the narrow road leads towards the Elan Valley, where the Cambrian Mountains glow with colour. The dark orange bracken, the soft green moss and the grey rocks were illuminated by a pale sunlight just as we turned the corner, where suddenly we could see water from the reservoir cascading over Caban Coch Dam into the valley far below. A few miles further on, we had a picnic beside tranquil waters where sportsmen fish for trout and salmon, and the sun glinted on the copper roof of the central control tower of yet another spectacular dam, at Pen-y-garreg, where pines almost enclose the sides of the mountain road right up to the level of the reservoir.

At Devil's Bridge the brightly-painted coaches of the narrow gauge Vale of Rheidol railway take holidaymakers on a scenic drive, and the series of waterfalls plunge down a deep wooded chasm into the river Mynach. The Devil himself was said to be the earliest guardian of the gorge and the lower bridge was built by the Abbot of Strata Florida in the twelfth century so that his monks could reach their sheep pastures on the opposite banks. In Tudor times, robbers who lived in a cave below the gorge preyed on travellers, so that in the eighteenth century a higher bridge was built, followed by a third, where today sightseers gather before climbing down a pathway cut into the rock to approach the thundering waterfalls.

At Aberystwyth, a cliff railway takes visitors aloft to see the view of Cardigan Bay, and the seafront curves round to a promontory where a graceful winged Victory holds a wreath of laurels. The hotels and boarding-houses with their nineteenth-century detailing of clubs carved in the stone, or panels of pebbles inset into the frontage, are painted yellow, emerald green, orange, and café-au-lait.

The King's Hall, with a clock tower, used for concerts and dances, is pale apricot, Avondale House is mustard and white, the bay windows of Victoria Terrace are decorated by columns on each of the three storeys and the Bellevue Royal Hotel is the pink of seaside rock. As you walk along the promenade, you are stimulated by this exciting mixture of colour, and the cry of the seagulls, the bracing air which fills your lungs, the blue and white shelter and the well-kept amusement arcade on the pier all give a holiday atmosphere to this university town.

The stone cottages at the end of North Parade, the neat houses of Castle Terrace and the unusual architecture in the High Street, where rusticated stone highlighted with panels of red and yellow brick, dormer windows with painted gables, and inlaid arches of yellow brick which surround the front doors, emphasise the care and pride taken by Welsh architects, using local materials, to include interesting details in these intimate streets.

Wales is famous for farmhouse holidays, and I sampled traditional Welsh cakes and Welsh pastries at a fifteenth-century timbered black-and-white farmhouse near Newtown, where my hostess entertains visitors from Holland, Germany and France who want to ride, fish or shoot rabbit and wild duck. Not far away, at Welshpool, Powys Castle, of red gritstone, with bastions and outer walls of the thirteenth century, stands high above the seventeenth-century formal gardens with three descending terraces which have views across the Severn to the English border.

For Wales is a land of farms and castles, of mountains, rivers and rocky streams, where Palaeolithic man hunted 12,000 years before Christ. Herodotus recorded that the Celts originated from the region of the Upper Danube, and the Roman garrisons in Wales did not completely subdue the Welsh-speaking Celts who lived in the mountains.

In AD 500 Cunedda proclaimed himself King of North Wales, and this heralded a period of Celtic revival, during which St David reformed the Welsh church and enrolled priests and monks from the families of princes and chieftains. In subsequent centuries the Welsh people were harassed by Vikings, Saxons and Norsemen, until Hywel the Good drew up laws, codified the system of land tenure and maintained peaceful relations with the English Athelstan of Wessex. Despite all his efforts to secure peace a decisive battle with the English in 1039 was a victory for Gruffyd ap Llywelyn, who after further battles became the ruler of Wales. Later

Sweet innocence

Welsh graveyard monuments

the Normans marched into Wales by the Roman roads, built an extensive line of castles and collected tolls from the inhabitants, but allowed them to farm the less fertile land under Hywel's laws.

In 1255, Llywelyn the Last became an ally of the border barons, and was acknowledged by Henry III in the Treaty of Montgomery as the Prince of all Wales. Edward I later attacked the country and, when Llywelyn sued for peace, he stripped him of his gains, but allowed him to marry Eleanor, daughter of Simon de Montfort, in Worcester Cathedral. Four years later, Llywelyn followed the initiative of his brother who had seized Hawarden Castle, advanced on King Edward's possessions in mid-Wales, and was killed near Builth Wells. Another Welsh leader was Owain Glyndwr, cousin to the Tudors, who in 1400 was proclaimed Prince of Wales. He established Welsh as the official language and for a few years assembled a Welsh Parliament in Machnlleth and Harlech. When English forces, released from the wars in France and Scotland, advanced in

View of the River Ithon

strength, he was defeated, but vanished into the woods and was never found.

In 1457, Henry Tudor, grandson of Queen Catherine of Valois and son of the Earl of Richmond, was born to the fourteen-year-old Margaret Beaufort in Pembroke Castle. After seven years' imprisonment during the siege of Harlech Castle, he was taken to France at the age of fourteen for safety by his uncle, the Earl of Pembroke, brother to Henry VI. In 1485 he returned to Wales, landing with 2,000 men on the shores of Milford Haven. After the defeat of Richard III he ascended the English throne as Henry VII. He appointed Welshmen as bishops and sheriffs in Wales, and amply rewarded his Welsh supporters.

Today Welsh culture, the Welsh language and Welsh religion flourish, and increasing numbers of travellers visit this remarkable country. In 1982, as the Pope landed at Cardiff airport, a male voice choir sang *There's a welcome in the hillsides*. There is a welcome also in the towns, in the villages, in the farmhouses and in the cities, where the poetry, the tenacity, and the courage of the Welsh people, in times of travail or triumph, have always shone like a beacon over the Welsh hills.

BATH SPA

O NE IS ALWAYS SUSPICIOUS of exaggerated praise. Statements like 'See Naples and die', or 'You must not miss the Taj Mahal by moonlight', are apt to send one in the opposite direction, and it was only the writings of Sacheverell Sitwell, whose architectural judgements are invariably right, which inspired me to set off to see Santiago de Compostela in Spain. At the time I was a guest of the Spanish Government, attending a seminar in Madrid in connection with European Architectural Heritage Year, and, as part of the Spanish contribution to that exercise devised to boost the restoration of historic buildings in Europe, our hosts wanted to show delegates the old castles which they had saved from ruin and converted into Paradors, the Government Hotels. We had a choice of journeying to the south, to Granada or Seville, both of which I had already seen and greatly admired, or to the north. It was then that I embarked, not by water at Tarsus, but on a coach which was obliged to effect interminable turns round the bends of the road which led us via Benavente and León to Santiago, hardly altered over the years.

The square, which is composed of the soaring west front of St James the Less, the Town Hall designed in 1682 by a French architect and the fifteenth-century Parador, named after Los Reyes Católicos Ferdinand and Isabella, is a sight unrivalled in the world. I will always be grateful to Sacheverell Sitwell. Yet despite my intense enjoyment of the architectural wonders of Spain, France, Egypt and Brazil, of Austria, Switzerland and Germany, of Denmark and Sweden, Portugal, Italy and Thailand, I still consider that Bath is one of the most beautiful cities I have ever seen.

The first, misty view, half-hidden in a dip of the Avon valley, is a tantalising promise of pleasure to come. The restrained architecture of Percy Place, the artisan East Hayes and Kensington Cottages, the dwellings sloping upwards in Brunswick Street, the simple two-storey buildings of Chatham Row, all prepare visitors for the grander houses in Queen Square or St James's Parade. For this is not a place where there is only one star turn, or where the occasional historic building remains like poor Hogarth's house near the roundabout in the Great West Road, isolated in the midst of factories like a living person unclothed and sent to Coventry. The Georgian builders of Bath understood that major architecture must have the right setting.

Pulteney Bridge

I have always remembered the sets of a performance of Carmen I once saw in Verona, where Seville, the city where the story takes place, was represented by a row of Italian seventeenth-century houses, and in the centre of the stage, the cigarette factory from which the sultry Carmen emerged was an important pedimented mansion modelled on drawings by Palladio. That tribute paid by the stage designer to their local celebrity, born at nearby Padua, and who did so much work at Vicenza, could well be copied in reverse by architects today who force unsuitable neighbours into a street or square already occupied by buildings of distinction.

In 1754 John Wood the elder designed the Circus in Bath. The stunning sight of this complete circle of houses, in honey-coloured Bath limestone, cleaned, repaired, lived in and enjoyed, captures the imagination. There are paired columns on each storey – Tuscan, Ionic, Corinthian – and the careful detailing of the frieze, with its motif of leaves, helmets, and entwined snakes; the balustrade which runs along the top, surmounted by stone acorns as a tribute to Prince Bladud; and above all the fact that this is a complete entity, undisturbed by any intrusive elements, makes this an essay in town planning comparable to the Place Vendôme in Paris or the Place Stanislas at Nancy.

Brock Street, deliberately plain, where the lettering, as at Santiago, is incised into the stone, links the Circus with Royal Crescent, a great sweep of formal architecture with giant Ionic columns, perched above Royal Victoria Park, from where distant views of Combe Down are just discernible over the tops of beech and

Music in the Pump Room

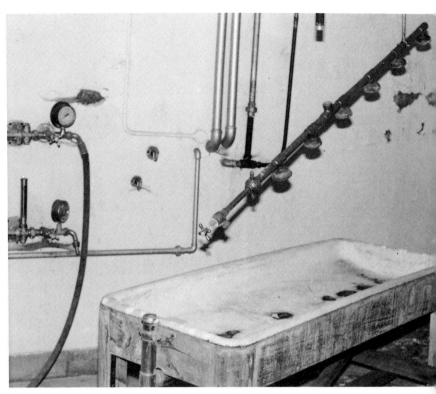

Above Invalids' shower (*left*) and treatment room at the Cross Bath
Below left Bath chair. *Below right* Changing cubicles at the Old Royal Bath

horse-chestnut trees. For Bath is also a city of trees and flowers, of steep cobbled alleys, of stepped pavements and intriguing lanes where café tables and tubs of flowers vie for a place, where young and old pause to shop for cheeses or patisseries, old prints, paper weights, water colours or children's toys.

The colonnades of Bath Street, with its hanging lanterns, were once thronged with sedan chairs and elegant company making for the King's and Queen's Baths, before the discovery of the Roman Baths, now considered one of the finest monuments north of the Alps. Today the adjacent Pump Room provides luncheons, music and countless glasses of spa water, and in 1983 work begins on a new international medical spa for this city, to which early sufferers from rheumatism travelled to seek relief, from the damp marshlands of Somerset, and from Gaul and the Western Empire.

Bath was recognised as a spa even before the Roman era, and coal from the Forest of Dean was burned on the altar of Sulis, the Celtic goddess of the hot springs. In 500 BC, Prince Bladud, a Celt of the West Country, was banished from his father's court as a leper and wandered alone, tending a herd of pigs which he fed with acorns. The pigs also developed sores and lesions, but one day, after wallowing in some warm mud in a valley, their skin started to heal. The prince then bathed in the hot water and was promptly cured. He returned to his father's court, and when he became king, pronounced Bath to be a sacred place.

The Roman Baths were discovered by chance in 1878 when the City Engineer, pursuing a leak, found a large overflow drain leading to a Roman reservoir beneath the existing King's Bath. Subsequent excavation over the last two centuries has revealed a series of rooms containing five baths, two swimming-pools, hypocausts, steam rooms, cooling rooms, and the Great Bath, with its floor of lead from the Mendip mines where stone steps lead down into the water. The spring was considered a holy place, and gem stones, vessels of pewter, bracelets, a gold carving, brooches and thousands of coins had been thrown in to placate the Gods.

After the Romans had gone, the baths in later years were in the care of the Benedictine monks who used them to help sick people and pilgrims who came to the town. In 1616 Anne of Denmark, wife of James I, arrived in Bath to seek a cure for her dropsy, and travellers from far afield continued to visit the hot springs even during the Civil War. After the Restoration, the physician to Charles II publicly recommended the waters, and in 1668 Bath was visited by the ubiquitous Samuel Pepys. But it was Queen Anne in 1702 who started the fashion for this small West Country town, and it was transformed into a smart watering place by a showman who proved to be an efficient organiser – Beau Nash. Born in Swansea and educated in Carmarthen, he went to Jesus College, Oxford, and subsequently became a soldier, lawyer and addict of the gaming tables, before deciding to seek his fortune in Bath. Once there, he ingratiated himself with the authorities, and was after a short period appointed Master of Ceremonies. He began without delay to regulate the social activities of the town. First he had to round up the vagrants, scare off the highwaymen, persuade the council to improve the roads and light the

Statues around the Roman Bath
The Roman Bath

streets, clean up the lodgings and fix fair charges. He encouraged the building of an Assembly Room, a theatre and a Pump Room and engaged musicians from London. He drew up a set of rules which banned swords, together with their attendant evil of duelling, improved manners generally, and started to raise money for a Mineral Water Hospital for the poor. Even the nobility obeyed his edicts governing dress and behaviour, and Bath entered a new phase.

Daniel Defoe and Sarah, Duchess of Marlborough, became frequent visitors, coffee-houses flourished, and balls, assemblies, lectures on art, and cockfighting were patronised by the Beau Monde. Mr Gainsborough charged five guineas for a portrait, Mr Lawrence much less. New arrivals were greeted by 'merry bells', for which they paid according to their rank, and female patients bathed in the King's Baths up to their necks in hot water, wearing jackets and petticoats of brown linen and chip hats.

Then, as now, people went shopping in the area near the Abbey Churchyard, pausing to admire Bath Abbey, started in 1499 by Bishop Oliver King, secretary to Henry VII, on which angels climb up the façade, and then strolled on over the wide paving stones to Abbey Green, where an ancient plane tree gives shade in the summer. Today there are still specialist shops for stamps, linen, sheepskins and knitwear in Old Lilliput Alley, just off the Green, and others down a few steps to Lilliput Court. Perhaps they stopped at Sally Lunn's, built in 1480, the oldest

Stall Street

Bath Abbey

house in Bath, where the recipe for her traditional cakes was found in the wall over the fireplace. There is still an open fire in the welcoming parlour on the first floor, and table-cloths of pink flowered cotton. The delicious patisseries are filled with apples or almonds, the torte of walnut sponge soaked in brandy is covered with a layer of coffee and chocolate mousse, and Sally Lunn cakes, resembling a toasted brioche, are eaten with gentlemen's relish, cinnamon butter, or jam and cream.

Visitors patronised the circulating library at 43 Milsom Street, where they read the London newspapers, bought writing paper and borrowed quill pens to write invitations or billets-doux. Today the long-established Jollys, with granite pillars supporting the entrance and brass lettering on the lower part of the bow windows, the colonnaded front of Richard Shops, and the handsome façade of Barclays Bank make this the most elegant shopping street in Bath.

But who could resist the chance to shop on Pulteney Bridge, built over the Avon in 1774 by Robert Adam; to buy antiques, flowers or a glass of wine in Margaret's Buildings; just to gaze at the serpentine curve of Somerset Place, or to walk down Lansdown Crescent, where sheep graze nearby on the mossy banks, and the houses have arched fanlights and lampholders of delicate wrought iron.

But this is not only a city for a fine day, when you can explore the alleys and

Royal Crescent

lanes near Northumberland Place, or admire General Wolfe's house in Trim Street, with its cartouche of a helmet, flags and arrows over the front door. There is a Museum of Costume, where you can see a smock with black-work embroidery of 1580; a court dress of silver tissue worn in 1660, with a collar of Venetian point lace; embroidered stomachers, pockets and coifs; paste buckles and pattens, with their overshoe which protected the slippers of fragile brocade. There is a kirtle of green satin with coral stripes, a dress of Spitalfields silk made by the Huguenot silk weavers who fled to England in 1685 after the Revocation of the Edict of Nantes, woven with saffron and dark blue flowers on a background of turquoise. There are knitted caps for babies threaded with glass beads, and, for dolls, straw hats trimmed with flowers and tiny gloves of blue glacé kid. This comprehensive collection has clothes of different centuries right up to the present day.

From the Carriage Museum in Circus Mews, landaus and curricles can be hired in the summer to take concert-goers to supper after hearing Bach and Vivaldi in the Assembly Rooms, and the Waggonette is used for sightseeing in the town. There is a fast two-wheel Regency Curricle, which was pulled by two pairs of horses, a

Front door in Lansdown Crescent

Ironwork on an old butcher's shop off St James's Parade

Reflection in a window in Lansdown Crescent

Bath facade

A narrow boat on the River Avon

View to the lake and Palladian bridge at Prior Park

Dormeuse of 1810 with a folding bed, a red and black Four-in-Hand once driven by Jennie Jerome, a baker's delivery van, and a Road Coach of 1839 which plied from Charing Cross to Rochester carrying passengers both inside and out. There is a collection of harness ornaments, and the brass footwarmers covered with carpet for the cold and hazardous journeys of those days recall Guy de Maupassant's classic story of snobbishness and ingratitude, *Boule de Suif.*

Best of all, I loved the Camden Works Museum, a memorial to Jonathan Burdett Bowler, brass founder, engineer and mineral water manufacturer, who never spent money unless as an absolute necessity and never threw anything away. As a result you can see his Machine Shop, first established in Southgate Street in 1872, where the pipe threader, the vertical drill and the lathe of 1870 were originally powered by steam, then gas, and now still work on electricity. In the pattern shop, the

Previous pages Prior Park

components of Mr Bowler's design would first be made in wood, then cast in the foundry. The finishing shop has tools for chasing and fettling, and treadle lathes, rather like an old-fashioned sewing machine, were used to trim away the bits of unwanted metal before the final polishing. There is an ingenious illuminated sign made of hollow iron piping, through which gas could run, emerging at intervals through perforated openings, to be an effective, although dangerous, means of advertising a shop or an event; and an unusual stove for heating flat-irons and those with curved bases for frills and ruffles, thought to have been sent to Mr Bowler for mending, which was the custom in thrifty Victorian times, before the advent of the throw-away society.

Among the old bills is an invoice for a soda-water machine for £14.9s.4d., and this was part of the equipment for his production of mineral water. All the original labels exist for Hop Stout, Cherry Ciderette, Hot Tom and Raspberryade, and there are numerous glass codds bottles containing marbles which acted as a cork, and quantities of wooden crates branded with his name. Some unusual early bottles have rounded ends and were stored upside down before the invention of patent closures ensured that the fizz did not escape. The most popular product was ginger beer, brewed in large vats where the ginger would be broken up in the grinder at one end. The large stoneware jars in which it was sold hold more than two gallons. There is the carbonating pump, of Mr Bowler's own design, and a crown corker from America.

The office has one of the earliest Oliver typewriters of 1907, a gas light, slates where items for an account were first recorded, and apprenticeship papers itemising details of a seven-year contract. You can also see the firm's coloured advertisements, and calendars which were given to regular customers at Christmas.

Many museums, however interesting, have to be content with scraps or fragments, but Mr Bowler's highly successful business, which did not close until 1969, can be seen in all its minute detail, and is an object lesson, even for those who attend sophisticated business schools, of a small Victorian enterprise which succeeded on the basis of prompt and reliable service, careful workmanship, honesty and thrift.

An invention of our own time can be seen at the Royal Photographic Society. This is a Hologram, an artistic design photographed on to a special emulsion painted on glass. When lit by a beam of parallel light from the front or the back, subjects such as an engraved glass vase or the inside of a turbine appear to protrude from the surface, the exact opposite to Tenniel's Alice as she stepped through the looking-glass. This process was used in the film *Star Wars*, and is a revolutionary technique which would have amazed Monsieur Lerebours of Paris, whose camera of 1845 is also on view, together with early Daguerrotypes. One portrays a serious lady with ringlets wearing checked gingham, and another, coloured by hand in 1848, is of Lord Cockburn, Secretary of State for Scotland. An amusing toy of the 1850s shows a badger about to take a photograph of a roguish female kitten.

How can we resist, while in Bath, a visit to the newly-restored Theatre Royal, built by George Dance the younger in 1805. Carl Toms has recently created on the ceiling a fantasy of grisaille like delicate gold filigree which centres on a giant chandelier. The panels which decorate the Dress Circle, shaped as rectangles, circles or diamonds, are also painted in the beige and gold grisaille, and the walls covered with raspberry striped silk, the seats of damson plush, and the carpet with medallions in these two shades make a setting like an expensive jewel-box for performances which attract audiences from far afield. The panelled bar, with copies of Victorian gaslamps and a clock inlaid with brass, the velvet stage curtains, the box office and a number of seats have all been endowed by donors wishing to support this major effort.

In Bath it is impossible to stay indoors for long, when there is still so much to gaze at and admire. The view of Bath Abbey as you come down Lansdown Road; the Sham Castle floodlit at night; the window canopies like open shells in Orange Grove; the arched fanlights on Bath Spa Station, built by Brunel; and the panorama from the height of Mount Beacon, make this a city for all seasons and all tastes, which Jane Austen used as a background in her books, but where it is not easy for mere mortals to stay in the foreground in competition with so much architectural splendour.

Most splendid of all is Prior Park, the brooding dream palace with its massive Corinthian colonnade, set on the southern slopes of Bath. Built by Wood for the remarkable Ralph Allen, a Cornishman by birth who became Postmaster of Bath, a brilliant businessman, a quarry owner, and son-in-law of General Wade, remembered for his suppression of the Jacobites, Ralph Allen was also the patron and associate of both John Wood the elder and his son, and over a period of years they collaborated to create the squares, streets and crescents which are so memorable in this city. At Prior Park, Alexander Pope, Garrick, Henry Fielding and William Pitt would gather to discuss art, literature and politics in the home of a man who had made a fortune through his own efforts, and was a generous benefactor to the entire community.

The house stands today above hundreds of stone steps contained by curved balustrades topped at intervals by urns with spiral carving which lead the eye down into the valley where the Palladian bridge appears to guard a toy lake. Beyond, on the hillside, are tier upon tier of houses built of honey-coloured Bath stone from the quarries at Combe Down which Ralph Allen had developed, and from which the stone was conveyed to the Avon, then shipped to Bristol, London and the major English ports.

Enterprise and ingenuity thus conjured up the dream which beguiles us today, and this palace, realised by a successful Georgian entrepreneur, seems to epitomise the enchanting combination of beauty, wit, sense and sensibility which has enabled Bath to survive as one of the world's most fascinating cities.

Roof of an old butcher's shop off St James's Parade

BIBLIOGRAPHY

Cheltenham Spa

BLAKE, Steven and BEACHAM, Roger, *The Book of Cheltenham*, Barracuda Books, Buckingham, 1982.

COX, W. L. and MEREDITH, R. D., *Haunted Cheltenham*, Gloucestershire County Library, Gloucester, 1982.

FINBERG, H. P. R., *The Gloucestershire Landscape*, Hodder & Stoughton, Sevenoaks, 1975.

PAKENHAM, Simona, *Cheltenham*, Macmillan, London, 1971.

ROLT, L. T. C., *The Dowty Story* (Parts 1 and 2), Leo Cooper, London, 1963.

RYDER, T. A., *Portrait of Gloucestershire*, Robert Hale, London, 1972.

VEREY, David, *The Buildings of England – Gloucestershire: The Vale and the Forest of Dean*, Penguin, London, 1976.

Woodhall Spa

GREATER LONDON COUNCIL, *Blue Plaques*, Greater London Council, London, 1971.

PEVSNER, Nikolaus and HARRIS, John, *The Buildings of England – Lincolnshire*, Penguin, London, 1970.

Buxton Spa

DEVONSHIRE, Duchess of, *The House: A Portrait of Chatsworth*, Macmillan, London, 1982.

GLADWYN, Cynthia, *The Paris Embassy*, Collins, London, 1976.

HAMMOND, Reginald J. W., *Peak District*, Ward Lock, London, 1976.

HEAPE, R. Grundy, *Buxton under the Dukes of Devonshire*, Robert Hale, London, 1948

MEE, Arthur, *The King's England – Derbeyshire*, Hodder & Stoughton, Sevenoaks, 1969.

PEVSNER, Nikolaus, *The Buildings of England – Derbyshire*, Penguin, London, 1978.

PORTEOUS, Crichton, *Portraits of Peakland*, Robert Hale, London 1963.

RESEARCH SOCIETY OF DEVONSHIRE HOSPITAL (Committee of), *Mineral Waters of Buxton*, Derbyshire Printing Co., Buxton, 1929.

SIMPSON, I.M., *The Peak District Rocks and Fossils*, Unwin Paperbacks, London, 1982.

TRESH, Dr, *Buxton as a Health Resort*, C. F. Wardley, Buxton, 1883.

WILLIAMS, Ethel Carleton, *Companion into Derbyshire*, Methuen, London, 1948

Royal Tunbridge Wells Spa

BOYLE, John and BERBIERS, John L., *Rural Kent*, Robert Hale, London, 1976.

CHURCH, Richard, *The County Books – Kent*, Robert Hale, London, 1966.

CROUCH, Marcus, *Kent*, B. T. Batsford, London, 1966.

DAVIS, Terence, *Tunbridge Wells: The Gentle Aspect*, Phillimore, Chichester, 1976.

JONES, Edgar Yoxall, *A Prospect of Tunbridge Wells*, Lambarde Press, 1964.

MAVOR, Elizabeth, *The Virgin Mistress*, Chatto & Windus, London, 1964.

MEE, Arthur, *The King's England – Kent*, Hodder & Stoughton, Sevenoaks, 1969.

NEWMAN, John, *The Buildings of England – West Kent and The Weald*, Penguin, London, 1970.

PEACOCK, David and CHAPMAN, Frank, *Tunbridge Wells Sketch Book*, Perspective Press, 1978.

SAVIDGE, Alan, *Royal Tunbridge Wells*, Midas Books, Speldhurst, 1975.

WEBB, William, *Kent's Historic Buildings*, Robert Hale, London, 1977.

WRIGHT, Christopher, *Kent Through the Years*, Batsford, London, 1975.

Droitwich and Malvern Spas

FRASER, Maxwell, *Companion into Worcestershire*, Methuen, London, 1939.

HAVINS, Peter J. Neville, *Portrait of Worcestershire*, Robert Hale, London, 1974.

HOLYOAKE, Arthur V., *Dear Little Droitwich*, Market Place Press, 1977.

HOUGHTON, F. T. S., M.A., F.S.A., F.G.S., *The Little Guides – Worcestershire*, Methuen, London, 1922.

LEES-MILNE, J., *Worcestershire – A Shell Guide*, Faber & Faber, London, 1944.

MEE, Arthur, *The King's England – Worcestershire*, Hodder & Stoughton, Sevenoaks, 1968.

MIDDLEMAS, Keith and BARNES, John, *Baldwin*, Weidenfeld & Nicolson, London, 1969.

PARROTT, Ian, *Elgar*, Dent, London, 1971.

PEVSNER, Nikolaus, *The Buildings of England – Worcestershire*, Penguin, London, 1970.

REED, William H., *Elgar as I Knew Him*, Victor Gollancz, London, 1936.

WAITE, Vincent, *Malvern Country*, Dent, London, 1968.

WHITLEY, W. T., *The Story of Droitwich*, Droitwich Guardian Office, 1923.

WYCHAVON DISTRICT COUNCIL, *Wychavon District Official Guide*, Home Publishing Co., 1975.

Strathpeffer Spa

COOPER, Derek, *Skye*, Routledge & Kegan Paul, Henley-on-Thames, 1970.

DAICHES, David, *Charles Edward Stuart – The Life and Times of Bonnie Prince Charlie*, Thames & Hudson, London, 1973.

FINLAY, Ian, *The Highlands*, Batsford, London, 1963.

GORDON, Seton, *Highlands of Scotland*, Robert Hale, London, 1952.

GRANT, James Shaw, *Highland Villages*, Robert Hale, London, 1977.

HAMMOND, Reginald J. W., *Complete Scotland*, Ward Lock Red Guide, London, 1980.

LISTER, John, *The Scottish Highlands*, Bartholomew, Edinburgh, 1978.

QUIGLEY, Hugh, *The Face of Britain – The Highlands of Scotland*, Batsford, London, 1936.

SIMPSON, W. Douglas, *Portrait of Skye and the Outer Hebrides*, Robert Hale, London, 1973.

WEINER, Christine, *Skye – A Travellers' Guide*, Grasshopper Press, Huntingdon, 1979.

Harrogate Spa

EDWARDS, Tudor, *Discovering Britain – Yorkshire*, Faber & Faber, London, 1978.

HARROGATE W. E. A. LOCAL HISTORY GROUP, *A History of Harrogate and Knaresborough*, Advertiser Press, 1970.

HAYTHORNTHWAITE, W., *Harrogate Story*, Dalesman, Lancaster, 1954.

LODGE, Eric, *Yorkshire Dales*, Yorkshire Dales Tourist Assoc., 1977.

LOWTHER, Kenneth E. and HAMMOND, Reginald J. W., *The Yorkshire Dales*, Ward Lock, London, 1980.

MITCHELL, W. R., *Haworth and The Brontës*, Dalesman, Lancaster, 1981.

PATMORE, J. A., *Atlas of Harrogate*, Corporation of Harrogate, 1963.

PEVSNER, Nikolaus, *The Buildings of England – Yorkshire: The West Riding*, Penguin, London, 1967.

PILL, David, *Yorkshire: The West Riding*, Batsford, London, 1977.

TATE, W. E. and SINGLETON, F. B., *A History of Yorkshire*, Phillimore, Chichester, 1967.

WALKER, Harold H., *Harrogate's Past 1884–1959*, Harrogate Borough Council, 1959.

Royal Leamington Spa

BURGESS, Alan, *The County Books – Warwickshire*, Robert Hale, London, 1950.

CLARKE, H. G., *Royal Leamington Spa – A Century's Growth and Development*, The Counter Press, Leamington & London, 1947.

HICKMAN, Douglas, *Warwickshire – A Shell Guide*, Faber & Faber, London, 1979

OLLARD, Richard, *This War without an Enemy*, Hodder & Stoughton, Sevenoaks, 1976.

PEVSNER, Nikolaus and WEDGEWOOD, Alexandra, *The Buildings of England – Warwickshire*, Penguin, London, 1960.

Llandrindod Wells Spa

GARDNER, Don, *Discovering Mid-Wales*, John Jones, Cardiff, 1978.

HAMMOND, Reginald J. W., *Complete Wales*, Ward Lock, London, 1976.

HASLAM, Richard, *The Buildings of Wales – Powys*, Penguin, London, 1979.

LOCKLEY, R. M., *Wales*, Batsford, London, 1967.

MORTON, H. V., *In Search of Wales*, Methuen, London, 1952.

SYLVESTER, A. J., *Life with Lloyd George*, Macmillan, London, 1975.

VAUGHAN-THOMAS, Wynford, *Wales*, Michael Joseph, London, 1981.

WALES TOURIST BOARD, *Wales: Castles and Historic Places*, 1974.

Bath Spa

BATH CITY COUNCIL, *Yesterday's Tomorrow – Conservation in Bath*, Fyson, Bath, 1976.

COYSH, A. W., MASON, E. J. and WAITE, V., *The Regional Books – The Mendips*, Robert Hale, London, 1977.

EASTERBY, Denis G., *Bath Official Guide Book*, Charles Woodward, Devizes, (published annually).

HADDON, John, *Portrait of Bath*, Robert Hale, London, 1782.

LITTLE, Bryan, *Bath Portrait*, The Burleigh Press, Bristol, 1980.

LITTLE, Bryan, *Portrait of Somerset*, Robert Hale, London, 1976.

MASON, Edmund J. and MASON, Dorrien, *Avon Villages*, Robert Hale, London, 1982.

PEVSNER, Nikolaus, *The Buildings of England – North Somerset and Bristol*, Penguin, London, 1958.

ROLFE, Wilfred E., *Somerset and Dorset*, Letts Motor Tour Guides, 1970.

SMITH, R. A. L., *Bath*, Batsford, London, 1944.

WINSOR, Diana, *The Dream of Bath*, Trade & Travel Publications 1980.

WORSKETT, Roy, GUNTON, Hugh and REDSON, Ronald V., *Saving Bath*, Bath City Council, 1978.

General

ADDISON, William, *English Spas*, Batsford, London, 1951.

DARTMOUTH, Countess of, *What Is Our Heritage?*, Her Majesty's Stationery Office, London, 1975.

FOSS, Arthur, *Country House Treasures*, National Trust/Weidenfeld & Nicolson, London, 1980.

LOCAL MEDICAL COMMITTEES (Compiled from reports of), *The Spas of Britain*, Pitman Press, Bath, 1925.

MORRIS, Christopher (Ed.), *The Illustrated Journeys of Celia Fiennes*, Macdonald, London, 1982.

SITWELL, Sacheverall, *British Architects and Craftsmen*, Batsford, London, 1945.

INDEX

Page numbers in *italic* refer to the illustrations.